Making Library Websites Accessible

PRACTICAL GUIDES FOR LIBRARIANS

About the Series

This innovative series written and edited for librarians by librarians provides authoritative, practical information and guidance on a wide spectrum of library processes and operations.

Books in the series are focused on describing practical and innovative solutions to a problem facing today's librarian and delivering step-by-step guidance for planning, creating, implementing, managing, and evaluating a wide range of services and programs.

The books are aimed at beginning and intermediate librarians needing basic instruction/guidance in a specific subject and at experienced librarians who need to gain knowledge in a new area or guidance in implementing a new program/service.

About the Series Editors

The **Practical Guides for Librarians** series was conceived and edited by M. Sandra Wood, MLS, MBA, AHIP, FMLA, librarian Emerita, Penn State University Libraries from 2014–2017.

M. Sandra Wood was a librarian at the George T. Harrell Library, the Milton S. Hershey Medical Center, College of Medicine, Pennsylvania State University, Hershey, PA, for over thirty-five years, specializing in reference, educational, and database services. Ms. Wood received an MLS from Indiana University and an MBA from the University of Maryland. She is a fellow of the Medical Library Association and served as a member of MLA's Board of Directors from 1991 to 1995.

Ellyssa Kroski assumed editorial responsibilities for the series beginning in 2017. She is the director of Information Technology at the New York Law Institute as well as an award-winning editor and author of 36 books including *Law Librarianship in the Digital Age* for which she won the AALL's 2014 Joseph L. Andrews Legal Literature Award. Her ten-book technology series, *The Tech Set* won the ALA's Best Book in Library Literature Award in 2011. Kroski is a librarian, an adjunct faculty member at Drexel and San Jose State University, and an international conference speaker. She has just been named the winner of the 2017 Library Hi Tech Award from the ALA/LITA for her long-term contributions in the area of Library and Information Science technology and its application.

Titles in the Series edited by M. Sandra Wood

1. *How to Teach: A Practical Guide for Librarians* by Beverley E. Crane
2. *Implementing an Inclusive Staffing Model for Today's Reference Services* by Julia K. Nims, Paula Storm, and Robert Stevens

3. *Managing Digital Audiovisual Resources: A Practical Guide for Librarians* by Matthew C. Mariner
4. *Outsourcing Technology: A Practical Guide for Librarians* by Robin Hastings
5. *Making the Library Accessible for All: A Practical Guide for Librarians* by Jane Vincent
6. *Discovering and Using Historical Geographic Resources on the Web: A Practical Guide for Librarians* by Eva H. Dodsworth and L. W. Laliberté
7. *Digitization and Digital Archiving: A Practical Guide for Librarians* by Elizabeth R. Leggett
8. *Makerspaces: A Practical Guide for Librarians* by John J. Burke
9. *Implementing Web-Scale Discovery Services: A Practical Guide for Librarians* by JoLinda Thompson
10. *Using iPhones and iPads: A Practical Guide for Librarians* by Matthew Connolly and Tony Cosgrave
11. *Usability Testing: A Practical Guide for Librarians* by Rebecca Blakiston
12. *Mobile Devices: A Practical Guide for Librarians* by Ben Rawlins
13. *Going Beyond Loaning Books to Loaning Technologies: A Practical Guide for Librarians* by Janelle Sander, Lori S. Mestre, and Eric Kurt
14. *Children's Services Today: A Practical Guide for Librarians* by Jeanette Larson
15. *Genealogy: A Practical Guide for Librarians* by Katherine Pennavaria
16. *Collection Evaluation in Academic Libraries: A Practical Guide for Librarians* by Karen C. Kohn
17. *Creating Online Tutorials: A Practical Guide for Librarians* by Hannah Gascho Rempel and Maribeth Slebodnik
18. *Using Google Earth in Libraries: A Practical Guide for Librarians* by Eva Dodsworth and Andrew Nicholson
19. *Integrating the Web into Everyday Library Services: A Practical Guide for Librarians* by Elizabeth R. Leggett
20. *Infographics: A Practical Guide for Librarians* by Beverley E. Crane
21. *Meeting Community Needs: A Practical Guide for Librarians* by Pamela H. MacKellar
22. *3D Printing: A Practical Guide for Librarians* by Sara Russell Gonzalez and Denise Beaubien Bennett
23. *Patron-Driven Acquisitions in Academic and Special Libraries: A Practical Guide for Librarians* by Steven Carrico, Michelle Leonard, and Erin Gallagher
24. *Collaborative Grant-Seeking: A Practical Guide for Librarians* by Bess G. de Farber
25. *Story-Time Success: A Practical Guide for Librarians* by Katie Fitzgerald
26. *Teaching Google Scholar: A Practical Guide for Librarians* by Paige Alfonzo
27. *Teen Services Today: A Practical Guide for Librarians* by Sara K. Joiner and Geri Swanzy
28. *Data Management: A Practical Guide for Librarians* by Margaret E. Henderson
29. *Online Teaching and Learning: A Practical Guide for Librarians* by Beverley E. Crane
30. *Writing Effectively in Print and on the Web: A Practical Guide for Librarians* by Rebecca Blakiston
31. *Gamification: A Practical Guide for Librarians* by Elizabeth McMunn-Tetangco
32. *Providing Reference Services: A Practical Guide for Librarians* by John Gottfried and Katherine Pennavaria
33. *Video Marketing for Libraries: A Practical Guide for Librarians* by Heather A. Dalal, Robin O'Hanlan, and Karen Yacobucci
34. *Understanding How Students Develop: A Practical Guide for Librarians* by Hannah Gascho Rempel, Laurie M. Bridges, and Kelly McElroy

35. *How to Teach: A Practical Guide for Librarians, Second Edition* by Beverley E. Crane
36. *Managing and Improving Electronic Thesis and Dissertation Programs: A Practical Guide for Librarians* by Matthew C. Mariner
37. *User Privacy: A Practical Guide for Librarians* by Matthew Connolly
38. *Makerspaces: A Practical Guide for Librarians, Second Edition* by John J. Burke, revised by Ellyssa Kroski
39. *Summer Reading Programs for All Ages: A Practical Guide for Librarians* by Katie Fitzgerald
40. *Implementing the Information Literacy Framework: A Practical Guide for Librarians* by Dave Harmeyer and Janice J. Baskin

Titles in the Series edited by Ellyssa Kroski

41. *Finding and Using U.S. Government Information: A Practical Guide for Librarians* by Bethany Latham
42. *Instructional Design Essentials: A Practical Guide for Librarians* by Sean Cordes
43. *Making Library Web Sites Accessible: A Practical Guide for Librarians* by Laura Francabandera
44. *Serving LGBTQ Teens: A Practical Guide for Librarians* by Lisa Houde
45. *Coding Programs for Children and Young Adults in Libraries: A Practical Guide for Librarians* by Wendy Harrop
46. *Teen Fandom and Geek Programming: A Practical Guide for Librarians* by Carrie Rogers-Whitehead

Making Library Websites Accessible

A Practical Guide for Librarians

Laura Francabandera

PRACTICAL GUIDES FOR LIBRARIANS, NO. 43

ROWMAN & LITTLEFIELD
Lanham • Boulder • New York • London

Published by Rowman & Littlefield
An imprint of The Rowman & Littlefield Publishing Group, Inc.
4501 Forbes Boulevard, Suite 200, Lanham, Maryland 20706
www.rowman.com

Unit A, Whitacre Mews, 26-34 Stannary Street, London SE11 4AB

All figures created by Laura Francabandera

British Library Cataloguing in Publication Information Available

Library of Congress Cataloging-in-Publication Data Available

ISBN 978-1-5381-0822-2 (pbk. : alk. paper) | ISBN 978-1-5381-0823-9 (ebook)

∞™ The paper used in this publication meets the minimum requirements of American National Standard for Information Sciences—Permanence of Paper for Printed Library Materials, ANSI/NISO Z39.48-1992.

Printed in the United States of America

This book would not be without the wholehearted support of my husband, Brandin, whose unflinching belief in my ability pulls me up when it all gets too much. You are the perfect partner for a lifetime of adventures.

To my children, Judah and Elijah, to show them what it looks like for a woman to be a mother and yet still focus on her career. May you grow up expecting women to do anything they want.

To those who work tirelessly for equity and accessibility but whose voice is unheard. You deserve a place at the table.

Contents

Preface

You may initially think that since we are librarians (and not web programmers) that website accessibility shouldn't apply to us. After all, there are people who do that kind of stuff for a career. Fair enough, but as librarians, it is also within our purview to ensure equal access to information. Now that much of that information is online, it is within our duty of care to ensure that information is accessible to all people—not just an able few.

Making Library Websites Accessible is a book that tries to bridge this gap in library and information science by offering a wide range of reference information about online accessibility, the disabilities our patrons face, and practical steps we can take to make our patrons' access to information smoother and more easily accessed. As librarians, it is a part of our ethical responsibility to ensure that our information pathways meet our patrons' diverse needs. Meeting diverse needs may mean we expand our skill set to basic web programming. Just like a circulation librarian might need to learn Spanish to give better service to her Spanish-speaking patrons, librarians may also need to learn HTML in order to make our library websites and online databases navigable for patrons with disabilities.

Changing times mean that librarians need to change with them. Our patrons' needs have likely already changed, so it is our job to find out what those needs are, which ones are not being met, and how we can meet those needs. Library websites should be easy to access, easy to navigate, and easy to use. Accessibility is not just a "web designer's problem." It is everyone's problem to solve, and we all have to do our part.

Scope

Making Library Websites Accessible is a reference book that walks you through the planning and process of testing your library website for accessibility. It serves as a reference for library students, librarians, and library staffs who work with a website.

It is intended to be read in pieces as much as it should be read as a whole. While reading the book from cover to cover will give you a thorough grounding in all aspects of accessibility, it is intended to serve as ready reference that you can periodically return to as you go through the accessibility process.

This book is not a handbook on how to create websites or to learn how to code. There are plenty of how-to guidebooks for web programming skills. Rather, this book shows you the code snippets and examples that are specific to website accessibility.

Making Library Websites Accessible is segmented into thematic chapters, with each chapter being complete in and of itself. Each chapter includes a scenario in which a librarian might use the skills that are taught in that chapter in her daily work. The scenarios are intended to serve as thought-provoking hypothetical situations, and any resemblance to actual scenarios, people, or places are entirely unintended.

Organization

Chapter 1 sets the tone of the book by offering a strategic view of why website accessibility should matter to librarians. It covers what, exactly, we mean when we talk about website accessibility and just why it is so important to libraries and librarians.

Chapters 2–6 go into detail on the different categories of disabilities and the challenges patrons face when trying to access information online. These chapters serve as a primer to visual, auditory, cognitive, motor, and social disabilities. They are not exhaustive on the subject, nor do these chapters cover every permutation of every disability. Disabilities are a vast range of increments, and it is not the purpose of this book to make sure that you know the difference between each disability. What these chapters do tell you are the most common challenges your patrons with these particular disabilities face when they try to access your library website, along with the specific assistive technologies they use to overcome those challenges.

Chapter 7 briefly covers the most known laws and regulations, including the Americans with Disabilities Act and Section 508 of the Rehabilitation Act of 1973. It is not an exhaustive cover of every single law and regulation concerned with disabilities and accessibility; rather, this chapter covers the laws and regulations you are most likely to encounter as a librarian, especially if you work in a publicly funded library.

Chapter 8 delves lightly into the philosophy behind accessibility and the importance of creating an ethic of care as a librarian and advocating for the oppressed. It also outlines the three principles of the universal design for learning (UDL), so you can create content that is accessible before it even gets on the website.

Chapter 9 is the chapter most directly related to actual web programming because it describes the HTML, JavaScript, and other interactive items that are commonly inaccessible for disabled people. It also explains what WAI-ARIA tags are and why they are important for context-rich widgets, such as tab panels. Again, this chapter will not teach you how to code, but will give you accessibility-specific tools and snippets to use when you create websites.

Chapter 10 goes into depth describing how you can conduct your own website accessibility testing from scratch. It starts by explaining how to create a rationale, leads you through the planning stages, explains your options for testing, and gives examples for a sample accessibility test. You can find full sample accessibility test sheets in appendix A of the book.

Chapter 11 walks you through what to do and expect if you find accessibility issues on a library database or a website that isn't one of your own. It lays out a basic advocacy road map and gives you some central tenets of advocacy to keep in mind while you are working with the third party to make accessibility changes to the third party's website. It can be difficult working with library vendors, especially if they are large corporations, and keeping some of these tenets in mind will help your case be heard, even in the largest of businesses.

Finally, chapter 12 gives you some ideas to think about beyond accessibility. Once you're done with accessibility, the last chapter gives you the basics of some well-known usability heuristics by Jakob Nielsen, some principles of universal design, and introduces you to the person-centered approach. Each of these are interdisciplinary fields of study that relate to accessibility in many ways and can enhance your knowledge and practice of an accessible and usable library website.

CHAPTER 1

The Basics of Accessibility

IN THIS CHAPTER

- ▷ Definition of accessibility
- ▷ Types of accessibility challenges
- ▷ Inclusive design versus accessible design

What Is Accessibility?

WHEN PEOPLE TALK ABOUT "ACCESSIBILITY" they usually mean that disabled people can use or access a specific item. It is an umbrella term that relates to many different facets of everyday life. You most often run across this term in reference to physical things, like the width of an aisle in the supermarket or the availability of a wheelchair ramp into a doorway. You can find accessibility research in nearly every discipline; from music to architecture and from astronomy to the library. Put simply, an accessible website is one in which all people can access the same information.

A 2013 survey by the Centers for Disease Control and Prevention (CDC 2015) found that 22 percent of Americans (or one in five adults) have a disability of some sort. Regardless of the severity or type of disability, a significant portion of patrons often are unable to access online content. The American Library Association's Code of Ethics (ALA 2006) places equal access to information at the top of the list. The library's purpose is to offer access to information. Without accessible websites, the library fails in its mandate. Librarians must ensure that the websites their library creates, produces, and promotes are accessible to patrons of all abilities.

This book introduces you to the health conditions and challenges that patrons face while accessing online information and the assistive technologies they use to overcome those challenges. It also explains the basic HTML code that makes websites accessible

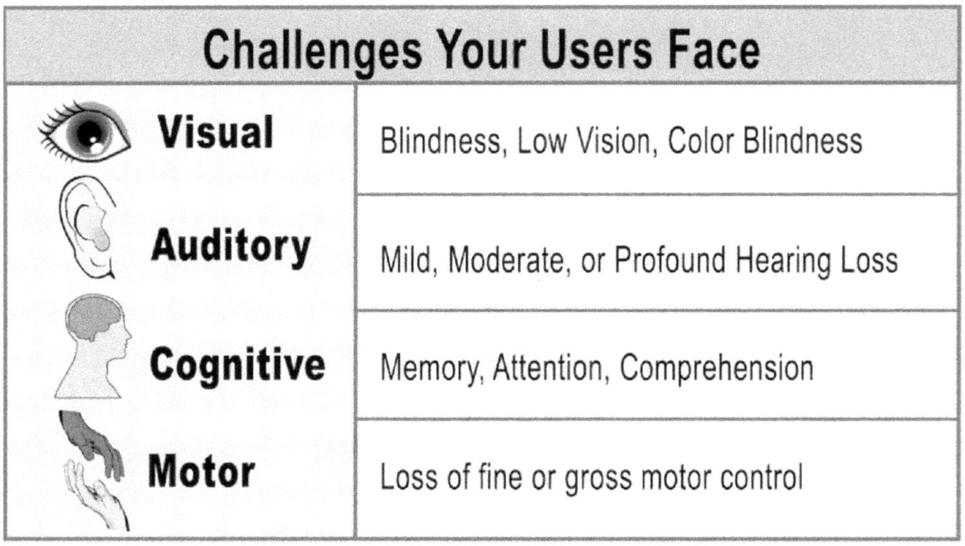

Figure 1.1. Accessibility challenges your patrons face

and gives you the tools you need to test websites for accessibility. There will be "real-life" scenarios in each chapter to help you understand what accessibility looks like in practice. This chapter gives you a brief overview of what accessibility is and how it relates to websites.

Types of Accessibility Challenges

There are many different types of disabilities and challenges that people can encounter when trying to access online content. This list is intended as an initial primer and is certainly not exhaustive. There are five main types of disabilities and challenges:

- Visual
- Auditory
- Motor
- Cognitive
- Social

It is important to note that within the broader group of each of the disabilities there are gradients and ranges. While all users are unique in the challenges they face, conforming to certain web standards will make it easier for them to access the information.

Visual

Visual disabilities and challenges are often what most people think of when confronted with web accessibility. If users can't see the computer screen, how can they access that information? Just as one person's vision acuity differs from another's, people with visual disabilities also differ: Some might simply have low vision and need to zoom their screen a bit, while others might be completely blind and rely on specialized software to read the entire website to them (AFB n.d.). Visual disabilities range from severe to non-serious but all are well served by building accessible websites.

Auditory

Users with auditory disabilities might seem like they could access information online just fine—they can at least read the computer screen. But they face similar struggles in accessing online content, especially in such a media-intensive era. Users may be completely deaf or may just suffer from slight to moderate hearing loss. They may have tinnitus or an inner ear infection, which also inhibits what they can hear. There is a range of disabilities and challenges in the auditory sense. Items of special concern for these users are videos, music, and integrated sounds. How will users know they are making an error if the only notification is a beep?

Motor

Users with motor disabilities often have trouble using a mouse or a keyboard (if they can use them at all), and as such must find other methods and technologies to move around online. In this case, it's not necessarily about the content of the web page, but ensuring that it is structured correctly and written using correct HTML code. If the code is messy or unorganized, then the assistive technologies will have trouble reading the website content correctly.

Users with motor or mobility disabilities often use the keyboard to navigate or may use voice-activated navigation. Certain online interactions, like drag and drop activities or forms, require careful consideration to include keyboard navigation.

Cognitive

Users with cognitive challenges may be able to access the web page but might struggle to understand the content. Some users with dyslexia may not be able to read the words on the screen easily, while other users might require a highly logical order or lower reading level for the text. The challenges that come with making accessible websites for cognitive disabilities rest mainly in the fact that people often do not fit into one or two easy buckets. Neurodiversity is a modern term for the age-old understanding that no two minds work exactly in the same manner (Sutherland 2016, 11). Making your websites accessible to users of all cognitive levels and disabilities requires you to make the content of your website accessible before it ever gets online.

Social

Finally, most people consider those physical and mental disabilities to be the end of accessibility, but limiting the challenges your users face in accessing online content to *just* physical and mental disabilities removes a large swathe of users who also cannot access websites. Users with social challenges encounter issues in accessing information online just as often as disabled users do, and disabled users disproportionately encounter these social challenges more than non-disabled users. How would you expect a user from a rural area with no internet at home to access library websites? What if a user from a different country wanted access to the information contained on your site—how could she translate it into her language? What about those users who cannot afford a personal computer?

Digital Divide

This is called the "digital divide" and is a well-known area of modern research. The thought behind this is that there are barriers to commonly used digital technology that limit people from accessing information; barriers like poverty, rural areas, access to fast internet, and other external forces (Newell 2011, 165). Users who face social challenges (economic, familial, and geographical issues) should also be considered when you are building accessible websites.

Regardless of the type or variation of disability that a user faces, making a website accessible benefits all users. There are users who are not classified into any of these sections (sometimes by choice) and have unknown challenges when accessing online content. The thought and time that you spend making a website accessible reaps direct rewards for these often vulnerable and overlooked users.

Inclusive Design versus Accessible Design

While this book focuses on making websites accessible, making the same website inclusive is a different research avenue. Inclusive design offers a more holistic approach because it understands that people don't always view the world the same way or come to a problem with the same set of skills and experiences.

Inclusive Design

Inclusivity is designing something for use but keeping in mind the lived experiences and valuable contribution from the often marginalized groups (Fletcher 2006). Inclusive design might be more concerned with content barriers rather than the technology barriers for certain groups of people, including things like the use of pronouns and gendered language or considering how a single parent might access or not access your content.

While there are many resources on creating inclusive content, this book will focus chiefly on the technology barriers to access.

Accessibility

Accessibility is what it says on the tin—making sure that all people can access a website regardless of their ability. This may include specific HTML coding, tags, labels, or customizable options.

DEFINITIONS

- Accessibility: Ensuring that all people have an equitable opportunity to access online information, regardless of disability
- Inclusivity: A method of designing and presenting information that can be consumed in a variety of formats by all people with a range of learning styles and abilities

WANT TO KNOW MORE?

If you want to learn more about inclusive design, see the section on universal design for learning in chapter 8. If you want to learn more about website programming and accessibility testing, see chapters 9 and 10.

Accessibility is mainly concerned with how people access the online information and ensuring that their access is equitable with the access of those without disabilities. Accessibility requires technological testing and some basic programming knowledge.

Key Points

This chapter gives you a brief overview of what accessibility is and how it relates to websites. Key points to remember:

- There are five main types of disabilities: visual, auditory, motor, cognitive, and social.
- Social challenges can also be known as the "digital divide."
- Accessibility is ensuring that all people have an equitable opportunity to access online information, regardless of disability.
- Inclusivity is a method of designing and presenting information that can be consumed in a variety of formats by all people with a range of learning styles and abilities.

References

AFB (American Foundation for the Blind). n.d. "Screen Reader Tips for Using the Web." Accessed March 26, 2017. http://www.afb.org/info/programs-and-services/daily-living/afb-senior-site-etips/see-all-featured-etips/screen-reader-tips-for-using-the-web/12345.

ALA (American Library Association). 2006. "Code of Ethics of the American Library Association." Advocacy, Legislation & Issues. July 7, 2006. http://www.ala.org/advocacy/proethics/codeofethics/codeethics.

CDC (Centers for Disease Control and Prevention). 2015. "Key Findings: Prevalence of Disability and Disability Type among Adults, United States—2013." Disability and Health. August 20, 2015. https://www.cdc.gov/ncbddd/disabilityandhealth/features/key-findings-community-prevalence.html.

Fletcher, Howard. 2006. "The Principles of Inclusive Design: They Include You." http://www.designcouncil.org.uk/sites/default/files/asset/document/the-principles-of-inclusive-design.pdf.

Newell, Alan F. 2011. "Design and the Digital Divide: Insights from 40 Years in Computer Support for Older and Disabled People." *Synthesis Lectures on Assistive, Rehabilitative, and Health-Preserving Technologies* 1, no. 1 (June 28): 1–195. doi:10.2200/S00369ED1V01Y201106ARH001.

Sutherland, Andrew. 2016. "Time to Celebrate Neurodiversity in the Workplace." *Occupational Health* 68, no. 11 (November): 11. https://ezproxy.rgu.ac.uk/login?url=http://search.ebscohost.com/login.aspx?direct=true&AuthType=ip,shib&db=c8h&AN=119550756&scope=site.

CHAPTER 2

Visual Disabilities and Assistive Technologies

IN THIS CHAPTER

- ▷ The range of visual disabilities, from eyestrain to total blindness
- ▷ Common screen reader and multimedia software
- ▷ Assistive technology for visual disabilities
- ▷ Accessibility issues with online text, tables, images, fonts, and colors

THIS CHAPTER WILL COVER THE MANY DIFFERENT TYPES of barriers that library patrons with visual disabilities may face as well as the technologies and strategies that they use to overcome these challenges. At the end of each chapter, there will be a list of resources and suggestions on where you can try these assistive technologies for yourself. The very best way to understand the difficulties that users face (except by asking them) is to experience it for yourself. In each of these "types of disability" sections, you will be given real-life scenarios, information about the variations of the disability and assistive technologies used.

When it comes to understanding the issues that a disabled user faces when accessing online material, the most important consideration is that there is no single correct way to make something accessible. Like all people, disabled users each come with their own preferences, biases, and quirks as to how they seek and access information online. Trying to lump them all into one bucket would be like trying to force all people to experience a sunrise or a symphony the exact same way.

Visual Disabilities

The issues that visually challenged patrons face greatly depend on the type and degree of disability. There is no hard limit to what constitutes a disability, but for the purposes of this book, a visual disability is defined as a patron having trouble reading or seeing the online content. This section will cover the different types of visual challenges that patrons may encounter as well as the assistive technologies that they use.

Blind or Low Vision

Users with low, moderate, or severe vision loss have trouble seeing the content on the screen. They also often have trouble using the mouse to navigate since they do not know where to click. These users often use the keyboard to navigate around websites and rely on assistive technology to tell them what is on the screen when they navigate. There are many different types of assistive technologies that visually disabled people use to read websites and computer screens.

Screen Readers

Screen readers are text-to-speech software that reads exactly what is on the computer screen out loud to the user, including computer icons, open programs, and web browser content. Screen readers can be quite expensive, running between $600 and $900 for the home editions. Some screen readers are open source and therefore low or no cost, but open source software typically comes with lower consumer support or help.

JAWS

The most common screen reader is JAWS, which stands for Job Access with Speech. This screen reader is compatible with Windows computers only, and it offers support for braille keyboards and language customization. JAWS is one of the most known screen readers and it comes bundled with DAISY, an accessible e-book reader.

NVDA

NonVisual Desktop Access (NVDA) is a free screen reader software developed by Non-Visual Access (NVA). NVA is a non-profit founded by two fully blind computer scientists who wanted to create an alternative screen reader to the expensive for-profit products. Due to the open source nature of this screen reader, it is ideal to use for accessibility testing by sighted web designers.

VoiceOver

Users who own an Apple computer may choose to use the Apple VoiceOver screen reader, which comes pre-installed on every Mac. Users can enable VoiceOver under the Accessibility section in the Preferences panel. VoiceOver generally contains the same functions as most other screen readers. The main difference is that VoiceOver is integrated with the computer operating system itself, so users are able to use it with all the Apple programs that come standard on their computers.

Orca

Orca is a screen reader for Linux computers. It is provided as open source, so application and software developers are able to take it and extend its capabilities. It is easy and free

COMMON SCREEN READER SOFTWARE

- JAWS (Job Access with Speech)
- NVDA (NonVisual Desktop Access)
- Apple VoiceOver (Mac software)
- Orca (Linux software)
- WebbIE (Online browser software)

to download provided you have a Linux computer. The downside and risk to using open source software is that it is usually provided free of any warranty and users assume their own risks in installing and using the software. These open source projects can be useful if the user cannot afford the cost of mainstream screen reader software or an Apple computer.

WebbIE

A final type of screen reader software, like WebbIE, is web-based software so users can use it on any computer (not just their own) or take it along with them on a memory drive or USB stick. The benefits to this type of screen reader are the portability and affordability of the software. Once users get used to their screen reader software, it is convenient for them to be able to take it with them wherever they go.

Screen Readers in Libraries

Due to budget constraints, libraries often choose a free or low-cost screen reader software for their computers. Some libraries only install it on a single computer and point blind users to that particular computer, but that reflects a bias because not every user of screen readers is blind. You may not know which user needs a screen reader, so the most inclusive option would be to install one on every public computer in the library and ensure there is signage about the option at each computer.

It is easy to get lost in the array of options when it comes to choosing a screen reader, but it is important to keep in mind that the way that people use screen readers is generally the same regardless of which software they use. People find one voice that they like, they customize it, and they get used to it. They know its idiosyncrasies and its phrases of speech, they understand the commands, and they know what to expect. When a sighted user first tests a screen reader, it may seem awkward and difficult to understand or navigate, but that is simply because the sighted user is not used to it. The more experience you have with listening to screen readers and understanding how and why they read things the way they do, the better you can design a website for visually disabled users.

Skip to Content Links

One of the common issues for patrons who use screen readers is the tedium of listening to long lists of links, especially on a website navigation bar. Keep in mind that because a screen reader will read the same navigation list of links every time the patron navigates to a new page on that website, it is important to give the user control on when to skip those links. If a sighted patron is not interested in an entire list of links, he can choose just not to read them. Patrons who rely on screen readers have little choice.

When you are creating a web page navigation bar, it is vital that you include a hidden "skip to content" link, just for screen readers. Visually impaired patrons will usually look for this link first so they can get right to the content on the page instead of waiting for the computer to list all the navigation links.

Multimedia Players

In addition to screen readers (which read the content on a computer screen out loud) there are specific video and audio file players that were created for screen readers. The buttons on the video player are labeled specifically for the screen reader to read, there are customizable keyboard controls, the video player will pause the video if there is a secondary audio description running so it doesn't interact with the actual video audio, and so much more (Able Player n.d.). There are also audiobook and e-book formats created especially for disabled users.

The DAISY Digital Talking Book

The DAISY Digital Talking Book offers easy navigation via keyboard, screen reader access, choice of voices, and other accessibility options. At first glance audiobooks would seem like they were accessible enough—they do read the content out loud, after all. Audiobook players, however, are a completely different story. The audiobook player needs to be interoperable with screen readers and be voice or keyboard navigable to be fully accessible. What use is an audiobook if the screen reader cannot accurately read the controls?

Able Player

Able Player is an online video player built with accessibility in mind. It has video control buttons that are labeled specifically for screen readers and a robust keyboard control system. The video controls (Play button, volume, etc.) are in high-contrast colors and easily visible for low-vision users. The best part about Able Player is that it is open source and is free and relatively simple to use. As awareness of accessibility issues gains traction, there will be more and more software applications that are made specifically with screen readers and visually disabled users in mind.

Braille

Software, like screen readers and video players, is one thing, but visually disabled users also often need computer hardware specific to their needs. One popular item is a braille keyboard, so when users navigate a web page using the keyboard they can read the braille to know which keys to press. Screen readers expect the user to navigate via the keyboard (instead of a mouse), so the combination of a screen reader and a braille keyboard can be quite common.

Refreshable Braille Display

Some users may prefer to use a refreshable braille display, which is a specialized flat surface placed in front of the user and connected to the computer. The software reads what is displayed on the computer and sends it to the refreshable braille pad, which then renders it in braille on the flat surface so the user can read it. When the computer screen changes, the braille refreshes to display the new content. Refreshable braille displays are often connected to a braille keyboard, so a computer set up for a blind or visually challenged user can be very complex and expensive. One reason the user may prefer a braille display instead of just listening to a screen reader is that it offers direct tactile information and the user can identify things like punctuation and spacing, whereas with a screen reader, the user is dependent upon its interpretation of the grammar (AFB n.d.).

Braille Keyboard

Braille keyboards are special keyboards with six buttons that correspond to the six braille places and additional computer keys like the space bar, Enter, and Delete. These keyboards plug in to a computer via USB port but do require special software to understand the braille input. Many blind users do use regular computer keyboards that have braille on the keys to let the user know which key is which. They can be rather expensive, so there are other options available like braille keyboard covers and braille overlay stickers to place on each key.

Braille in Libraries

One option that libraries may consider in an attempt to increase user accessibility is to offer a refreshable braille display for use at the library. Disabled patrons are often unable to afford the very devices intended to help them. Libraries are community centers that are well placed to offer this possibility to patrons. Libraries can also ensure the availability of accessible e-books or audiobooks as a regular part of acquisition and collection management.

Elderly People

Elderly people often struggle with low or reduced vision and can also benefit from the same accessibility standards. Older adults are one of the fastest growing population segments, so involving them as a stakeholder in accessibility is vital to their care and social inclusion as generations grow older (Frid et al. 2015, 5). Elderly patrons fall under many of the disabled categories, as vision, hearing, motor control, and mental facilities all decline with age. In addition to those disabilities, they have an added "digital divide" challenge because technology is often new and unfamiliar to them. Library programs and classes dedicated to helping elderly users navigate websites or learn about the assistive technologies they can use would be a great way to provide outreach to an under-served but growing section of the community.

Screen Magnification

Some users might be able to see just fine but still have difficulty reading text on computer screens. You might know this as "eye fatigue" or "eyestrain," and it is gaining traction as an ailment specific to computers and electronic screens (American Academy of Ophthalmology 2016). There are many reasons why sighted individuals might choose to use a screen reader or other assistive technology; perhaps it is simply more comfortable or maybe they have a medical reason to not strain their eyes. Regardless of the reason, many sighted people use assistive technology to access online content. These users might choose to use a screen reader or other text-to-speech tool, but they also may rely on screen magnifiers or a built-in zoom function.

Responsive Design

While zooming in on a website is easy and intuitive, it can cut off content from the pages of poorly designed websites. The most accessible websites reorganize the content of the page depending on the browser display size. The website will look different depending on whether the user is zoomed in; this is called responsive design (Petersen 2014, 4).

A common example of responsive design in practice is the difference between the desktop version of a website and a specially designed mobile version. Some computer magnifying and zoom tools only zoom text (so users aren't distracted by things they don't want), while other tools enlarge the entire page. There are also zoom tools that users can take with them on a USB memory drive so they can have the familiarity of their own personal software on any computer they use (WebbIE n.d.).

Fonts and Typography

There are specific fonts that are more difficult for low-vision users to see. These fonts typically fall under the umbrella of "serif fonts." Serif means the fonts have extra flourishes or strokes on the edges of the letters and are differing widths at different points on the letter (in a rather calligraphic way). These fonts include most of the traditional "typewriter-like" fonts, such as Times New Roman or Georgia. These extra strokes on the edges of the letters can interfere when low-vision users try to read the text on the screen, so most accessibility designers recommend using one of the "sans serif" fonts (meaning "without strokes"). These sans serif fonts (such as Arial or Verdana) are blockier, straighter, and much easier to read.

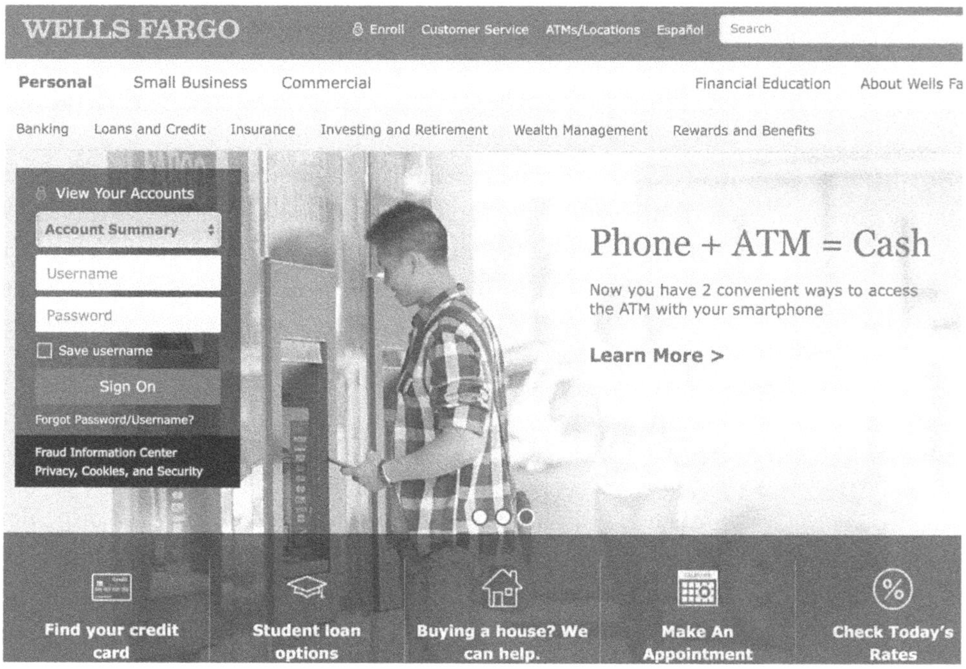

Figure 2.1. Responsive design in action: Wells Fargo desktop website

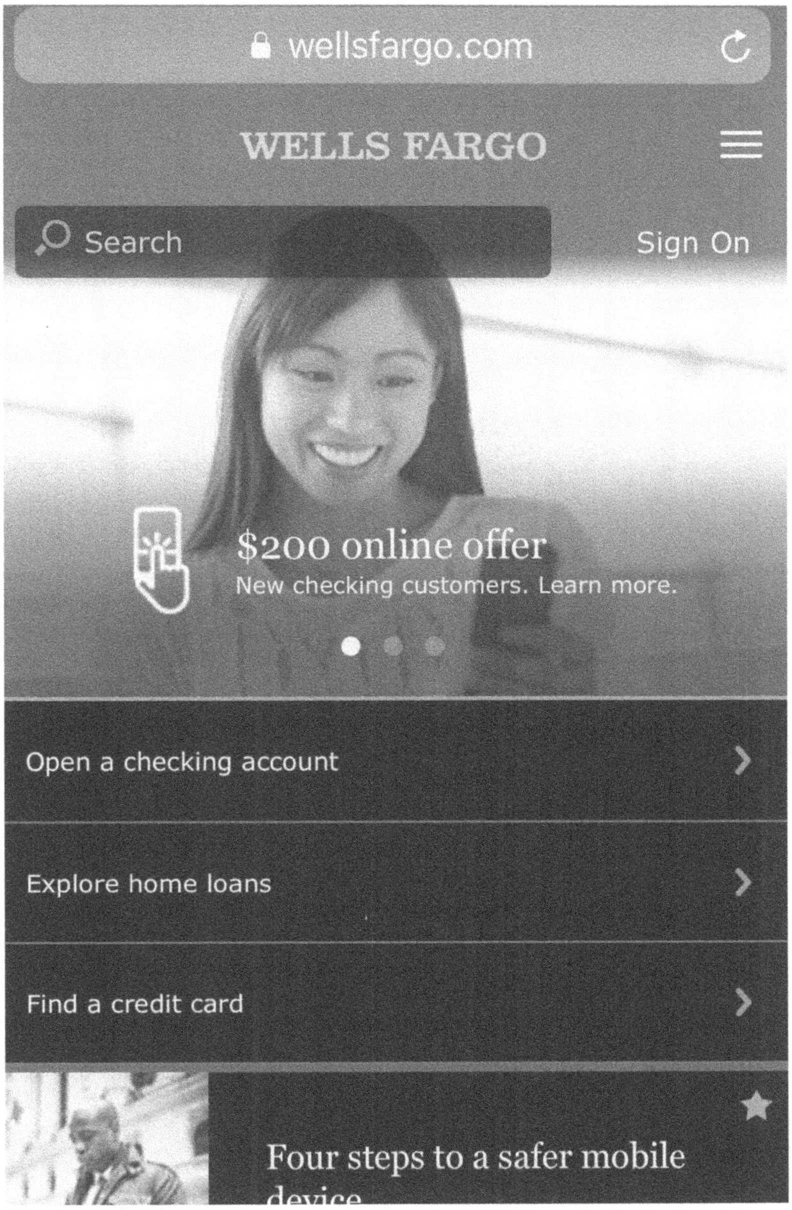

Figure 2.2. Responsive design in action: Wells Fargo mobile device website

Leading and Tracking

It is also important to understand the leading and tracking of the letters and how they impact the readability of the text. Leading is the height of the letters (from the bottom of the "y" to the top of the "b"), and tracking is the space between the letters (Pipes 2011, 172). If the leading is larger (taller, elongated letters) but the tracking is not enough (the letters are too close together), then the font will be nearly illegible to low-vision users. It works the other way around too—text can be difficult to read if the letters are too far apart or too short.

Color Contrast

Fonts also need to be placed against a background with sufficient color contrast. The best combination is black text against a white background. There are numerous options

DEFINITIONS

- Serif: Letters that have flourishes or strokes on the ends of the letters
- Sans serif: Letters without flourishes or strokes on the ends of the letters
- Leading: The height of the letters from the lowest descender to the highest ascender
- Tracking: The space between the letters

for combinations, like yellow text on a blue background or maroon text on a black background. The Web Content Accessibility Guidelines (WCAG) accessibility standards suggest a *minimum* color-contrast ratio for foreground text to background color of 4.5:1 (W3C n.d.). There are plenty of online and downloadable color checkers that verify the contrast ratio between two different colors strictly for the purpose of accessibility:

- The Paciello Group Colour Contrast Analyser
- WebAIM Online
- North Carolina State University Color Checker

Alternative Text for Images

Blind users often run into an issue perceiving images on web pages. Web designers (or anyone who puts images online) need to provide an alternative text for the screen reader to read. If no alternative text is manually given, the screen reader will either skip over the image or just say "graphic"—neither of which are helpful at all to the blind person trying to understand what is displayed on the web page. Images are a mix of autonomous meaning (the image by itself) and its meaning in relation to its surrounding text (the context) (Oregon State University n.d.). Alternative text for images should take the surrounding context into account to determine how much and what information a blind user would need.

Low Internet Speeds

Offering an alternative text is helpful to sighted users as well. There are many reasons why a sighted user might need alternative text on an image, but it most commonly occurs

REAL-LIFE SCENARIO

If an image of a cow in a field was placed on a page about farming, the image would likely just need minimal information, as its purpose is merely decorative (e.g., "A brown cow standing alone in a field"). If the same image of a cow, however, was placed next to another image of a cow in a section about bovine behavior, the image description or alternative text should explain what the cow is doing in each photo. Context is vital to understanding images in relation to the surrounding text.

when the patron is using a slow internet connection and his browser cannot process the images. When that happens, the browser displays a small clip art graphic and whatever the alternative text is for that image. The user will have no idea what the image was supposed to be if there is no alternative text.

Assuming that everyone has access to high-speed internet or the proper technology resources to process an image-heavy website is symptomatic of the privileged class in the digital divide. Many people do not have access to high-speed internet and so depend on alternative text in images as an integral part of their web browsing experience. Remember, accessibility helps more people than you would expect.

Decorative Images

Many web designers note that if the image is simply decorative that there should be a "null" description so the screen reader will skip over it. That is not necessarily true, and it reflects a sighted bias that is systemic to society in general. Every single image should have a description (even if it's just a purple curlicue around a white flower) because it is not the job of sighted people to regulate what is important for a blind user to understand—it is the blind user who determines the value of each image.

The best practice for alternative image text for decorative images is to give a general description of the entire image and then go into more detail only if the context calls for it, leaving the value interpretation to the end user.

Tables and Graphs

Tables, graphs, infographics, and other detailed images should be either linked to a full-screen image with explaining text, or include everything the user would need to know in the image description. If you are unable to link to a full-size image, then it is important to get all the information into the alternative text in a logical order. If you are adding the alternative text to a graph, the text will need to explain the context, not just the data points.

REAL-LIFE SCENARIO

Take a look at these two alternative texts for a graph and try to imagine what the graph would look like. Which one helps you visualize the graph more?

- Alt text #1: "A bar graph explaining the correlation between drunk driving accidents and time of night."
- Alt text #2: "A bar graph showing the correlation between drunk driving accidents and time of night. The horizontal x-axis is labeled 'Time of Night' with three times listed: 11 p.m., 12 a.m., and 1 a.m. The vertical y-axis is labeled 'Number of Accidents' with three numbers listed: 1, 2, and 5. The first bar shows that there was 1 accident at 11 p.m. The second bar shows that there were 2 accidents at 12 a.m. The third bar shows that there were 5 accidents at 1 a.m."

Social Media

One overlooked area where alternative image text is incredibly important is social media. Most social media platforms offer an image caption area for the user to add explanatory text, but not everyone uses it even when it's available.

Twitter is particularly difficult due to the 280-character limit on tweets. If you tweet an image or link to an image, you may not have room for a complete image caption. Twitter offers an accessibility function where you can compose an image caption up to 420 characters. The image description is invisible to sighted users but will show up for screen readers or refreshable braille devices. This option is only available on Twitter.com or the official mobile applications and is not a part of third-party Twitter schedulers like Hootsuite or TweetDeck. You will need to investigate the image description options of whatever social media application you use to determine if it satisfies the alternative text need.

If you post images on Facebook or other social media platforms, you must provide a caption of the photo. These captions can be regular photo captions, but if you post a link to a news article, Facebook will typically show an image for the article if available. You will need to caption the featured image within the text of your post itself.

Color Blindness

Color blindness is a genetic trait that means an eye cannot perceive a particular color. The most common form is red-green color blindness, but there also is a blue-yellow form as well. Statistics show that up to 8 percent of men and 0.5 percent of women are red-green color blind, which means that the colors red or green are invisible or abnormal to them (National Eye Institute 2017).

Color blindness is particularly difficult in websites that rely on color (especially red or green color) as the only indicator of a particular meaning or message. This most commonly manifests as correct or incorrect markings on a form or quiz, web page alerts or warning popups, and colored text or buttons (WebAIM 2013). If you have a red button right next to a green button with no other information, a color-blind user will not know which button to select. If a library website relies on heavily visual information (such as book covers, icons, or search results), the surrounding information needs to supplement what is missing when the user cannot perceive color.

Key Points

Designing for accessibility is a continual process. You try to meet the known needs now, but keep in mind that you may still need to change the website at a later time. Key points to remember:

- Visual disabilities vary in severity and type.
- Patrons with visual disabilities often rely on screen reader software and zoom magnification to read website content.
- It is vital that website designers include alternative text for any graphic format, such as images, tables, colors, and graphs.
- Sans serif fonts are the most accessible.

Further Resources

Screen Readers

- JAWS: http://www.freedomscientific.com/Products/Blindness/JAWS
- VoiceOver: https://help.apple.com/voiceover/info/guide/10.12/
- NVDA: https://www.nvaccess.org/
- Orca: https://help.gnome.org/users/orca/stable/introduction.html.en
- WebbIE: http://www.webbie.org.uk/

Braille Technology

- The Chicago Lighthouse: https://www.lighthousetoolsforliving.com/Braille-NotetakersDisplays_c_134.html
- Perkins School for the Blind: http://www.perkinsproducts.org/store/en/39-braille-displays
- Sight and Sound: http://www.sightandsound.co.uk/hardware/braille-displays.html

Multimedia Players

- Able Player: https://ableplayer.github.io/ableplayer/
- The DAISY Digital Talking Book: http://www.daisy.org/daisypedia/daisy-digital-talking-book

References

Able Player. n.d. "Able Player." Accessed April 4, 2017. https://ableplayer.github.io/ableplayer/.

AFB (American Foundation for the Blind). n.d. "Refreshable Braille Displays." Accessed March 26, 2017. http://www.afb.org/prodBrowseCatResults.aspx?CatID=43.

American Academy of Ophthalmology. 2016. "Computers, Digital Devices and Eye Strain." March 1, 2016. Accessed March 26, 2017. https://www.aao.org/eye-health/tips-prevention/computer-usage.

Frid, Linnea, Alvaro García, Iker Laskibar, Aitziber Etxaniz, and Mari Feli Gonzalez. 2015. "What Technology Can and Cannot Offer an Ageing Population: Current Situation and Future Approach." In *A Multimodal End-2-End Approach to Accessible Computing*, edited by Pradipta Biswas and Carlos Duarte, 3–22. London: Springer. https://doi.org/10.1007/978-1-4471-6708-2_1.

National Eye Institute. n.d. "Facts about Color Blindness." National Institutes of Health. Accessed March 17, 2017. https://nei.nih.gov/health/color_blindness/facts_about.

Oregon State University. n.d. "Alternative Text for Images." Accessed March 26, 2017. http://oregonstate.edu/accessibility/alttext.

Peterson, Clarissa. 2014. *Learning Responsive Web Design*. Sebastopol, Canada: O'Reilly.

Pipes, Alan. 2011. *How to Design Websites*. London: Laurence King.

WebAIM. 2013. "Visual Disabilities: Color-Blindness." August 28, 2013. http://webaim.org/articles/visual/colorblind.

WebbIE. n.d. "WebbIE, the Free Web Browser for Blind People with Little or No Sight." Accessed March 26, 2017. http://www.webbie.org.uk/.

W3C. "Web Content Accessibility Guidelines (WCAG) 2.1." Accessed May 15, 2017. https://www.w3.org/TR/WCAG21/.

CHAPTER 3

Auditory Disabilities and Assistive Technologies

IN THIS CHAPTER

- ▷ The basics of deaf culture
- ▷ A range of auditory disabilities, from partial hearing loss to deaf-blindness
- ▷ Assistive technology for auditory disabilities, including video transcription and sign language
- ▷ Accessibility issues with multimedia, such as videos, audio files, and volume controls

Deaf Culture

BEFORE GOING INTO THE POSSIBLE CHALLENGES and assistive technologies that deaf people use, it is important to unpack important ideological differences in how deaf people identify themselves. Identity is complex, and how deaf people label themselves is even more so. The most common deaf identities are between *deaf* people (lowercase "d") and *Deaf* people (uppercase "D"). Deaf culture is the self-formed identity and worldview of individuals who consider deafness to not be a disability, but simply a different normal (Leigh 2009, ch. 1). They reject the label "hearing impaired" because they view themselves as completely whole (not disabled or impaired at all). They focus more on advancing sign language and other forms of deaf communication as a native language.

Deaf Identity

Deaf identity is highly collective, and members view themselves as part of an extended family. There can be ideological differences within deaf culture and, as with any community,

DEFINITIONS

- Deaf: Someone who identifies with Deaf culture and refuses the medical model of disability
- deaf: Someone who is medically deaf and uses assistive technology for hearing aids

there are outliers or those who leave the culture. For example, some deaf people may look down upon other deaf people who use assistive technology like cochlear implants or hearing aids. In the case of medical technology, there can be a sense of betrayal from those within deaf culture because they assume the deaf person has succumbed to the disability mind-set. When it comes to website accessibility, it is best left up to individual choice as to which technologies users find acceptable to use within their moral worldview.

Deaf identities are incredibly complex, and it needs to be known that not every deaf person uses assistive technology in the same manner, if at all. Throughout this book we will reference all deaf users as *deaf* (not *Deaf*) to encompass the broadest category of users, but please keep in mind the variations between users with auditory challenges. While the choice to use assistive technology is a personal one, this book will focus on all the different possibilities that deaf people are able to use if they so choose.

Auditory Disabilities

Users who encounter hearing difficulties rely heavily on captions and transcripts to understand videos and music content. These captions and transcripts must be robust enough so the user can understand the context of the scene. Is an actor laughing outside of the camera angle? If it is not written into the closed captions or transcripts, these users will not know that. This section offers a brief primer on deaf culture as it relates to web ac-

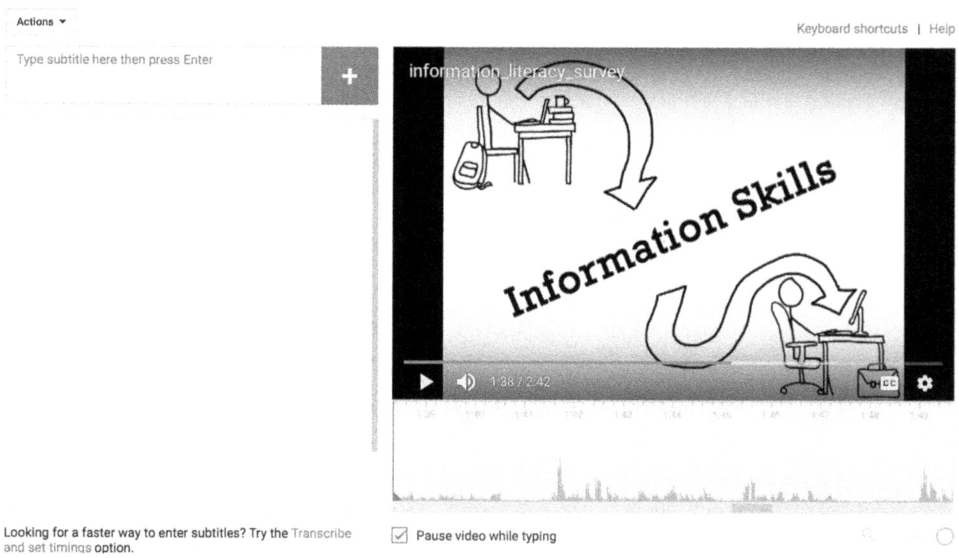

Figure 3.1. YouTube closed-caption and transcript creation website

cessibility. It also covers the difficulties that deaf or hard-of-hearing users will face when accessing online content, especially multimedia.

Deafness

When users are mostly or completely deaf, they rely on captions and transcripts to understand what sounds are being generated. This can apply to computers in general, where error sounds need to be accompanied by a popup error window, or to video or audio files on a web page. If a video is put online without captions or a transcript, the deaf user is left with lip-reading and body language interpretation to understand what is occurring. You should not assume that every deaf patron is skilled at lip-reading or interpreting body language.

Captions

Captions are the most common form of assistive technology and are used not only online but also on phones and televisions. Captions are the text boxes that show up at the bottom of a screen (or online video) and display the narration. Most common video players, like YouTube or Vimeo, offer the opportunity to add captions for your video. Many people choose to not upload captions and often cite the time it takes or the nature of the video as reasons why. Regardless of the reason for not uploading captions, the fact remains that a vast portion of online videos remain inaccessible for deaf users. It is incredibly important to caption any videos that you put online because it can be the only way that some users can access the content.

Captions can be open (always shown on the screen) or closed (users have the option to turn them on or off), but they are always synchronized with the audio (Hearing Loss Association of North Carolina n.d.). If users need more time to read something on the screen, they need to pause the video or rewind it to finish reading. One of the shortfalls of captions is this need to keep up with the narration, which can be really stressful. Another shortfall is that captions often only include the narration and not any of the ambient sounds, music, or other noises.

Transcripts

Transcripts are different methods to offer the same information as captions but in a more flexible form. Most transcripts allow for downloading so the user can keep a text copy to refer to later. A transcript shows the narration for the entire video at once, allowing users to take whatever time they need to read the transcript and to scroll back and forth easily. Transcripts can either be timed or untimed and synchronized or unsynchronized (Colorado State University n.d.). Timed transcripts tell the reader what time within the video

DEFINITIONS

- Closed captions: Users have the choice to turn the captions on or off.
- Open captions: Captions are always shown whether the user wants them or not.

REAL-LIFE EXAMPLE SRT FILE

```
1
00:02:17,000 --> 00:02:20,000
Senator, we're making
our final approach into Coruscant.

2
00:02:20,000 --> 00:02:22,000
Very good, Lieutenant.
```

the narration occurs, down to the second or millisecond, while untimed transcripts just give the block of text, without any time markers. Synchronized transcripts are those that highlight the sentence that is being said in the video so the transcript highlights move along in pace with the narration. A transcript can be any combination of these options, but synchronized, timed transcripts are ideal.

SubRip Transcript Format

A common form for transcripts, captions, and subtitles is a SubRip transcript (SRT). This transcript style offers specific rules about how each item should be formatted and timed. SRT files include four lines per transcript item: A number (for display order), a video time in milliseconds, the text, and a new line.

WebVTT Transcript Format

Another popular format that is used more specifically with subtitles and captions is Web Video Text Tracks (WebVTT) format. This style supports more flexibility in the design and style of the captions (like having the captions scroll up instead of completely changing) but also is more complicated to write because it includes HTML and CSS. WebVTT format also allows for language options and internal notes in the transcript file. The most basic form and easiest to write is the SRT format, which can be written in any basic text editor.

REAL-LIFE EXAMPLE WEBVTT FILE

```
00:02:17.000 --> 00:02:20.000 position:50% align:center
Senator, we're making
our final approach into Coruscant.

00:02:20.000 --> 00:02:22.000
Very good, Lieutenant.
```

Audio Descriptions

A final aspect of transcriptions that often gets overlooked is a full description of all the audio—not simply the narration. Many video creators think that putting up a transcript of the narration alone should be sufficient for deaf or hard-of-hearing users. This is a systemic bias against hard-of-hearing people because it assumes the logic that the hearing person knows what is important in the video and what is unimportant.

Transcripts should, therefore, also include all noise or audio (even if deemed irrelevant by the video creator), including music soundtrack, sound effects, off-camera noises, laughs, and any other sounds that are a part of the video or audio file. In the same way that sighted people should not determine which images are important for a blind user to see, hearing users cannot determine the importance of a particular sound to a deaf user. Valuations should be left up to the individuals with the disability to decide for themselves.

Sign Language

One consideration in making online multimedia accessible is to offer a sign language translation for any video or audio that you put online. As seen from the "Deaf Culture" section earlier in the chapter, sign language is often considered a native language for hard-of-hearing users and should be considered a part of language accessibility. In a 2015 user study (Kushalnagar et al. 2015, 835), researchers found that "out of 32 participants who knew ASL and English, only 3 students expressed a general preference for English in daily communication." Just as you would consider adding a Spanish language translation, you should also consider including a sign language translation to any multimedia.

The reason for considering a sign language translation is because English is commonly used as a second language for those who are severely or profoundly deaf from a young age. Most people are not as literate in a learned second language as they are in their native language. The speed of captions on videos requires a high (nearly native) level of English literacy to be able to keep up with the captions. Modern deaf education places the teaching emphasis on communication and learning, rather than speaking or specifically oral communication (Enns 2009, 4). This leads to a more native acquisition of sign language and leaves reading comprehension of English as secondary.

Sign Language Technology

The technology to automatically create sign language translations is still under development. Currently the only way to make a sign language translation is to film a sign language translator and then place it next to the audio content. There are companies that contract strictly for sign language translation for businesses, but they are still an on-demand and often expensive service. There have been inroads in automated sign language translation software, such as Microsoft Kinect for Windows, but those are mainly for use with software application developers—not website designers. At this time, the best and most cost-effective choice to offer a sign language translation video is to get a native signer to sign it for you.

Partial Hearing Loss

Users with partial hearing loss are usually able to get by on captions or transcripts, but there are specific accessibility issues that affect users with partial hearing loss.

Volume Controls

The most accessible multimedia players give users the option to control the volume of the audio. Hearing loss is a spectrum, so no two users' hearing will be at exactly the same level. It is important that users are able to change the volume of the audio independently of their own computer volume. They may have their computer volume set at a specific level but only need to change the audio level a small amount.

Volume controls generally are a standard feature in most video and audio players, but it is the website designer's responsibility to ensure the volume controls exist and that they work correctly.

Speed Controls

If users require extra time to decode and understand the narration, it is important that they can slow down the audio to a speed with which they are comfortable. When used in tandem with a timed transcript, this gives users complete control of the speed and pace in which they digest the material.

There are many accessible video players that offer speed control to the user, and the feature is becoming standardized on many mainstream media players as well. YouTube offers speed control in its new HTML5 video player, but it can be difficult to locate if you don't know it's there. The more accessible video players, such as Able Player, offer speed control as a visible setting on the main video control panel. If it is not obvious that the feature is available, it is likely that hard-of-hearing users will never know that they even have the option of changing the speed of the audio.

Unexpected Noises

The rest of the hard-of-hearing accessibility issues fall under the umbrella of "unexpected noises." For a hearing user, unexpected noises are often nothing more than a slight irritant. For hard-of-hearing users, however, noises such as background noise, unexpected warning beeps, or other distracting noises can easily overshadow the main audio.

There generally isn't software designed to help the users over the unexpected noises hurdle—rather, the issue must be solved in the design phase. When you are creating the video, pay particular attention to any background noise in the video itself. Are you in a busy city? A noisy park with lots of birds chirping? Is the air conditioner or fan on? Any sound that is tangential to the main audio can muffle the audio and distract users from what you want them to hear. Research has shown that hearing aids are often able to counteract and account for background noise (Dean and McDermott 2000, 139), but there is a significant portion of hard-of-hearing users that do not wear hearing aids and for whom background noise is a significant obstacle.

Autoplay

Users with hearing loss can often have trouble with video or audio files that are set to play automatically as soon as they get to the website. Not only is it confusing when they can't tell which section of the page the audio is coming from, but it can also startle them as they expect to have time to adjust their hearing aids.

For best accessibility practices, users should have complete control as to when and how their video plays, as this helps hearing and sighted users also. When in doubt, design the audio features for deaf and hard-of-hearing users, because that also is beneficial for hearing users at the same time.

Deaf-Blindness

Deaf-blindness is more than just the combination of someone being deaf and blind. It is a complex web of degrees of sight and hearing, which can make communication extremely difficult. Deaf-blindness is one of the most diverse disabilities because people can have a range of vision and hearing loss—no two deaf-blind people are exactly alike. People can be born deaf-blind or they can come into it later in life (known as secondary deaf-blindness). Deaf-blind people often struggle with secondary disabilities related to their deaf-blindness or its genetic causes (National Center on Deaf-Blindness 2008). They often have moderate to severe learning disabilities or other cognitive or physical disabilities.

Deaf-Blindness and Assistive Technology

Because there are varying degrees of vision and hearing loss in deaf-blind people, they often use the same assistive technology as other blind or deaf users, such as screen readers, braille devices, screen magnifiers, and so forth. There are extra devices that can give a more tactile impact for those with severe vision and hearing loss. There are signalers that users can connect to their computers that vibrate when they get a new email, switches that select items on a website, amplified headsets, and so much more.

When designing content, deaf-blind users will benefit if you follow accessible content and instructional design. For more information on how to design accessible content, please see the universal design for learning section in chapter 8.

Key Points

When it comes to making a website accessible to users with auditory disabilities, you must remember that not every deaf or hard-of-hearing user accesses technology the same way or with the same set of skills and knowledge. Key points to remember:

- Deaf culture is a unique social identity, and deaf people do not see themselves as disabled.
- Hearing loss is a spectrum, so you cannot expect all users to need the same volume level or set of tools.
- It is vital that website designers include captions and transcriptions for any multimedia file.
- Deaf-blindness is more than just the sum of its parts and often includes secondary disabilities.

Further Resources

Deaf Culture

- Laurent Clerc National Deaf Education Center: http://www3.gallaudet.edu/clerc-center/info-to-go/deaf-culture/american-deaf-culture.html

- Deaf Culture Centre (Canada): http://www.deafculturecentre.ca/Public/Default.aspx?I=294
- American Deaf Culture: http://www.americandeafculture.com/

Deaf-Blindness

- National Deaf-Blind Equipment Distribution Program: http://www.icanconnect.org/
- National Center on Deaf-Blindness: https://nationaldb.org/
- American Association of the Deaf-Blind: http://www.aadb.org/

References

Colorado State University. n.d. "Creating a Video Transcript: The ACCESS Project." Accessed March 26, 2017. http://accessproject.colostate.edu/udl/modules/multimedia/tut_video_transcript.php.

Dean M. R., and H. J. McDermott. 2000. "Preferred Listening Levels: The Effect of Background Noise for Moderate-to-Profoundly Hearing Impaired Aid Users." *Scandinavian Audiology* 29, no. 3 (August 8): 139–49.

Enns, Charlotte. 2009. "Critical Literacy: Deaf Adults Speak Out." *Exceptionality Education International*, no. 19, 3–20. http://ir.lib.uwo.ca/eei/vol19/iss2/2.

Hearing Loss Association of North Carolina. n.d. "Captions Definition." Accessed March 26, 2017. http://www.nchearingloss.org/caption.htm.

Kushalnagar, Poorna, Joan Naturale, Raylene Paludneviciene, Scott R. Smith, Emily Werfel, Richard Doolittle, Stephen Jacobs, and James DeCaro. 2015. "Health Websites: Accessibility and Usability for American Sign Language Users." *Health Communication* 30 (8): 830–37. doi:10.1080/10410236.2013.853226.

Leigh, Irene W. 2009. *A Lens on Deaf Identities*. Oxford: Oxford University Press. doi:10.1093/acprof:oso/9780195320664.001.0001.

National Center on Deaf-Blindness. 2008. "Overview on Deaf-Blindness." October 1, 2008. Accessed May 14, 2017. https://nationaldb.org/library/page/1934.

CHAPTER 4

Cognitive Disabilities and Assistive Technologies

IN THIS CHAPTER

- ▷ A range of cognitive disabilities, from dyslexia to autism spectrum disorder
- ▷ Methods to make websites more accessible for those with cognitive disabilities, including using natural language, clear wayfinding, and lowering the reading level
- ▷ Readability measurement instruments and software applications
- ▷ Assistive technology for cognitive disabilities, including reading and annotation software, colored glasses, and printing
- ▷ Photosensitive epilepsy

THIS CHAPTER WILL COVER THE MOST COMMON cognitive difficulties that people encounter when they access information online. The sheer breadth and depth of cognitive disabilities, disorders, and other challenges are too many to cover fully in this chapter. We will go over the most common issues that library patrons face when accessing online websites, as well as the assistive technologies they use to work around them. To find out how to build websites that benefit people with cognitive challenges, see the universal design for learning section in chapter 8. Mental health is an evolving science, and the more we learn about the brain and how it works, the better we are able to design accessible websites.

Instead of going into depth on the individual cognitive issues that people have, this chapter will focus on the actual challenges that people encounter in websites. It will pay special attention to the readability of text and to patrons with dementia and dyslexia.

Perception, Processing, and Comprehension

This broad set of difficulties relates to the challenges people face when perceiving, processing, and comprehending information, such as patrons with dyslexia or those on the autism spectrum. Users encounter a variety of issues but most of which can be resolved in the website design stage.

Reading Level

The reading level of text on a website should be at the lowest level possible for ease of use. According to the National Assessment of Adult Literacy, thirty million American adults have a below basic literacy level, which means they can only understand the most concrete tasks, while an additional sixty-three million have a basic, everyday-task level of literacy (National Center for Education Statistics n.d.). Such a large portion of society will struggle reading content on websites that is written at too high a level. This is doubly important when the information is vital—websites about topics such as health care, legal resources, and, yes, even libraries.

The best way to adapt the reading level of text on a website is to apply one or more of the readability scales. There are a variety of scales you can use:

- Flesch Reading Ease
- Flesch-Kincaid Scale
- Gunning-Fog Index
- SMOG Readability Formula (McGraw n.d.)
- Fry Readability Graph

One of the more common scales is the Flesch Reading Ease Score, which evaluates the complexity of a set of paragraphs. It compares the number of letters per word, words per

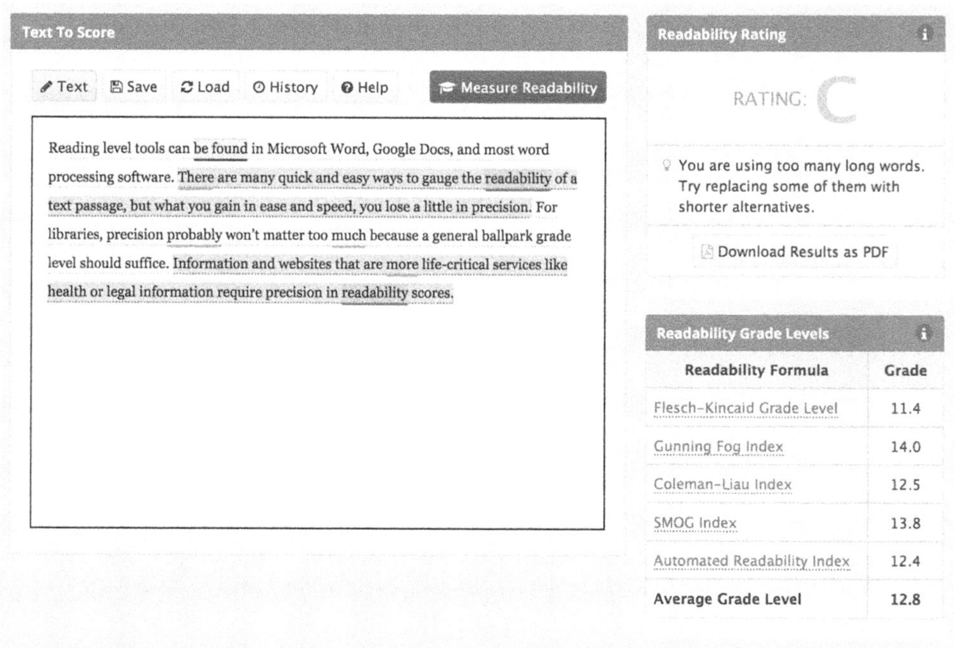

Figure 4.1. Screenshot of an online readability application

sentence, and sentences per paragraph and determines a readability level. You can then take this score and use the Flesch-Kinkaid Scale to turn it into a grade reading level (e.g., ninth-grade reading level).

Quickly Assessing the Reading Level

Reading level tools can be found in Microsoft Word, Google Docs, and most word processing software. There are many quick and easy ways to gauge the readability of a text passage, but what you gain in ease and speed, you lose a little in precision. For libraries, precision probably won't matter too much because a general ballpark grade level should suffice. Information and websites that are more life-critical services like health or legal information require precision in readability scores.

One application that helps to define the reading level of a chunk of text is an online website called Hemingway. You paste in a chunk of text, and it analyzes the readability and gives you grammar and spelling corrections, ease of sentence structure, and grade reading level. There are further resources available at the end of the chapter, but remember that websites and third-party applications can change rapidly.

For the users who struggle with illiteracy, however slight, their use of library websites will decrease dramatically if the text is difficult to understand. Simplifying the text on the web page by using shorter and less complex words and sentences can greatly increase its accessibility.

Jargon

As an extension of readability, jargon (or profession-specific language) is useful only within that particular profession. Librarians who go to a librarian conference should all be comfortable talking about "ILLs" and "OPACs," but a user of the library services has no grounding in these terms. To the average library patron, the library "OPAC" should just be called a "catalog," and the "ILL" could just be termed "borrow a book from another library." Here are some examples of jargon commonly found on library websites:

- OPAC
- ILL
- Databases or journals
- Electronic resources
- LibGuide

When making library websites accessible, librarians need to be aware of when and where library jargon is used, and make it a habit to switch it out with common language if at all possible. Patrons with cognitive difficulties have a hard enough time navigating natural language without the need to decode library jargon on top of it.

The best practice for librarians is to call a catalog a catalog (or better yet, a "book search") to aid this portion of patrons.

Reading Aids

For those users who need help reading and understand a block of text, there is plenty of assistive technology software that can help.

Screen Readers

Some users with cognitive disabilities are able to listen to someone else reading the words, but are unable to process the words themselves. People with disabilities like this often use screen reader software to read the website content aloud. Be aware, though, that screen readers read all the content on the computer screen, so some people may find them more confusing than helpful.

Text-to-Speech

Text-to-speech software applications are readers that read specific areas of the screen. In many cases, users highlight the portion of text they want to hear and the software reads it aloud. This is helpful for a range of cognitive disabilities because it allows users to decide what they need help with and what they can handle on their own.

Annotation Software

Some assistive technology allows users to annotate right over other applications on their computer screen. Some are stand-alone applications, and some are web-browser based. These annotation software applications allow users to make notes, organize their thoughts, circle words they don't know, and generally be more tactile with a website.

Some annotation software programs act more as bookmarking platforms, where users can tag websites, highlight content, and make notes, while others act as more as a physical corkboard, allowing users to add sticky notes and pin images. Annotation software is another way for users to make sense of website content in whichever method works best for them.

Tablets and Touch Screens

Some people with cognitive disabilities prefer touch interactions, as opposed to the remote feel of interacting with a website by moving a mouse. These people often use tablets or touch screens to interact with online content. Touch screens can either be a touch screen computer or a smartphone.

The benefits to touch screens are the immediacy and one-to-one relation of the touch and something happening on the screen. Many tablets and phones include software that make it easy to take screenshots and annotate them by drawing or writing on them. Tablets and touch screens are not typically thought of as assistive technology, but they are increasingly used for people with cognitive processing disorders.

Abstract versus Concrete Concepts

Many categories of mental disabilities relate to how people process abstract thoughts. Oftentimes, as with autism and other processing disorders, caregivers are strongly encouraged to use concrete examples and thoughts as often as possible. This is because the autistic person is often unable to differentiate between abstract and concrete statements (Moreno and O'Neal 2000). While metaphor is a very powerful tool and can help many people understand and recall a concept better, it leaves a portion of the users confused.

REAL-LIFE SCENARIO

A library in a rural town wanted to put a basic feedback survey on its website to ascertain the general emotional state of patrons when they left the library (e.g., happy, angry, or upset). The librarian thought that she might liven up the survey by using metaphors instead of emotions and used the following options: I'm on top of the world (for happy), I'm going to explode (for angry), I'm feeling blue (for upset). Many users liked this approach, but a small portion of users came to the librarian complaining that the survey made no sense to them; how can a person "feel" like the color blue? In this scenario, the librarian made a choice to value creativity over accessibility. A more accessible decision would have been to use the metaphors but also include the concrete translation underneath. By doing it that way she would have served all patrons, including the low-literacy and non-abstract patrons.

Dyslexia

People with dyslexia all process words and language differently. For some people, the words on the website or written page appear to move or to "swim," making it difficult to identify the intended word. For others, they have trouble remembering how to spell a word. Some people with dyslexia cannot read words on a computer screen at all—they need to print the information out in order to read it (American Dyslexia Association n.d.). There is no single specific way to design websites for accessibility with Dyslexic people.

Fonts and Typography

Since dyslexia most often relates to how people process and comprehend text, the best fonts for dyslexic people are sans serif fonts like Arial or Verdana. The straighter, blockier, and less complicated fonts are easier to read.

There are some study aids that offer a special dyslexia font that is optimized for people with dyslexia. The most important thing to remember when making a website accessible for patrons with dyslexia is to write clearly and use a clean, basic font.

Predictive Text

If you need users to type into a search box, it's important to offer some type of predictive text because many dyslexic people have trouble remembering how to spell certain words correctly. If you are unable to offer predictive text, then a semantic search engine would do the same job. A semantic search engine will return the page with no search results, but then prompt the user with search terms similar to the one she typed in: "You searched for 'beutiful,' did you mean 'beautiful'?"

Layout and Display

When making a website accessible for people with dyslexia, the most important consideration is how the text looks on the screen. Dyslexic users will all see the text

REAL-LIFE SCENARIO

A patron with dyslexia is trying to search for a digital resource in the library website search box, but it keeps coming up with "No pages found that match your search term." The webmaster installed a plug-in that offered predictive text, so next time this user could type in the first few letters and then select the term she wanted to search.

slightly differently, but there are some common user design strategies that will benefit all users:

- Minimize white space by using a single space after periods.
- Break up large blocks of text.
- Do not use justified alignment.
- Avoid moving or animated text.

Memory and Attention-Span Disorders

There are groups of disabilities that relate to how people store and use memories as well as how their attention is caught and kept. This section will briefly cover the challenges that people with memory and attention-span disorders face when accessing information online.

Dementia

With the growing elderly population, the percentage of adults with dementia and other memory disorders is ever increasing. The Alzheimer's Association (2017) notes that there are more than five million Americans with dementia, but at the current rate of growth there could be more than sixteen million by the year 2050. Libraries are a prime spot for catering to the needs of elderly patrons through many avenues: events, community, vital information, and so much more.

There are unique challenges that patrons with dementia face when accessing websites and information online. Dementia is most known for memory loss and a decrease in language and communication skills. There is not a lot of research done about how adults with dementia interact with websites, but due to the generalities of dementia itself, you can make inferences for accessible web design.

Loss of Memory

The loss of memory that comes with dementia is different for each person, depending on the severity and type of dementia present. People who have trouble remembering things need certain features on websites to help them stay on task.

Clear Navigation

Website navigation must be exceedingly clear and transparent for users with dementia. If page names and links are hidden within a dropdown navigation box, for instance, they may never realize it is there. The website navigation must be visible on the initial screen so users can identify where they need to go. People with dementia often have trouble planning and thinking linearly, and as such are often unable to follow a series of links to get to a page. Placing all the important and most used links on the front page will help patrons get where they need to go whether they can remember how to get there or not.

In general, online usability experts recommend no more than three clicks to get to any page on a website.

Wayfinding and Breadcrumbs

Some of the research that investigates how adults with dementia interact with websites has discovered that elderly users with Alzheimer's commonly were unable to group items into logical categories. This has vast implications for website design, particularly where navigation is concerned.

Typical website navigation groups pages into similar categories, which are then turned into navigation headers. If people with dementia and memory loss are unable to make that connection between grouped items, they will not know which category to choose. One way to mitigate this issue is to keep your navigation groups but turn them into boxes on the homepage with the title of each page visible and linked. That way users can scan all the links available instead of trying to figure out which navigation header will lead to it.

Breadcrumbs are another method of helping users find their way within a website ("wayfinding"). Breadcrumbs are the small, contextual navigational links that often show up below the navigation bar. It provides a path of linked pages for how you got to the current page. Typically, the breadcrumbs follow the navigation organization and can be helpful for users with dementia if they forget how their current page is grouped within the website as a whole.

Minimal Distractions

For users with dementia, it is easy to go off topic or become distracted. Websites that offer a plethora of information also offer many avenues of distraction, not just for users with dementia, but for all users. The internet can often feel a bit random, like when Alice fell into Wonderland. It is not uncommon to start out researching something specific online and then later find yourself on a completely different topic. You never planned to research the new topic, but a chain of links and interesting-looking pictures led you there. This

REAL-LIFE SCENARIO

An elderly patron with dementia finds herself looking at an online email form, but can't remember what the form is for. She looks for contextual clues to help determine the purpose of the form and find the website breadcrumbs. They look like: Home → About Us → Contact Us. That jogs her memory, and she is able to recall that she was going to email the library to ask a question.

chain of association can be much worse for users with memory disorders because their planning and processing center in the brain is damaged. They have trouble making a plan and sticking to it.

It is important to minimize distractions on websites so users can get from point A to point B as quickly and direct as possible. Fancy graphics, flashing animations, and advertisements are very distracting and lend little to the content of the website. All users are better served with a minimal-design website with few distractions.

Task-Focused, Familiar Language

One method for helping those with memory or attention-span difficulties is to design your website with task-focused, familiar language. When users interact with websites, they each come to the website with a mental model of what they expect will happen. Mental models of library websites, for example, could be something like this: Click on "catalog," search for book title, and view results. For those with a cognitive or neurological disorder, their mental models can become skewed or completely forgotten. Having things be task focused and in familiar language helps re-create their mental models.

Task-Focused Interactions

Making interactions on your website task focused is a best practice for general user-centered design. You want users to be able to quickly and easily find what they are looking for and to do what they need to do. Designing a website to be task focused centers users and their actions as the most important piece of the user-system interaction. This also helps users with cognitive disabilities because they often need clear directions on what they should be doing now and what they should do next.

This is easily seen in error messages on websites. If someone makes an error (enters a wrong digit in a username, clicks on a button he shouldn't, etc.), the resulting error message should be task focused—what did the user do and what should he do next.

REAL-LIFE EXAMPLE

If users enter the wrong password for their library account, they should receive an error message that is task focused. It should tell them what they did wrong and what they should do next. Here are three examples of error messages—example 1 is not helpful at all; example 2 at least gives a next step. Example 3 is very task focused and user centered because it contains three task-focused items: what happened to cause the error, a memory aid to help fix the error, and next steps.

- Example 1: "The username and/or password is incorrect."
- Example 2: "The password is incorrect. Re-enter your password and try again."
- Example 3: "You've entered the wrong password. Enter your password and try again. Remember, passwords must be at least 6 digits long and contain *both* a letter and a number. Click here to reset your password."

Natural and Familiar Language

To some extent, using natural (or "familiar") language sounds quite similar to avoiding jargon. You're still trying to make the text easier to read and understand. Natural language, however, is broader and further reaching than simply avoiding jargon. You can avoid jargon while still writing a complex sentence that is inaccessible to most of the population. There is a slight difference between familiar and natural language when it comes to technology.

Familiar Language

When a website uses familiar language, it uses the terms and verbal constructs users have of a task and mirrors that in the user interface. This can partly be described as avoiding technical jargon, but it also means that the website designers have spent time thinking about ways that users might approach and think about different tasks.

This is a key aspect of user design, where the user experience is at the center of website design: websites are created to work and look a certain way because that is easiest and most natural for the users. Many library websites are not created with the best user experience in mind, and that can be for many reasons. Often, library websites are just a sub-section of a larger city or county website and as such have no choice in the website design, but that is where advocacy is vital.

Familiar language is also important to use when thinking about the website interface buttons and navigation. These interface elements are instructional materials—they tell the users what to do and when (Usability.gov n.d.). If the instructions are unclear, users will not know what to do. This is doubly important for users with cognitive disabilities, as they require explicitly clear instructions and familiar language on buttons and interface items. The language used to do a task (e.g. using "Submit" for all form entry buttons, or "Go" for all search buttons) should stay consistent through the entire website. Users will become familiar with a task and will easily get confused if the language suddenly changes on a new page.

Natural Language

While similar to familiar language, natural language relates more to how computers process input from users. For library websites in particular, this means that the search boxes and catalog should be able to process natural language queries as well as structured Boolean search terms.

This is incredibly important for users with cognitive disabilities as they often cannot structure search terms and queries in a formal Boolean-type search equation, and more often use regular speech patterns in their searching habits. When users encounter a search box, they typically type in a regular question, rather than a formally structured search query.

All this is not to say that every library should get rid of formal Boolean searching, but it is important to understand how your patrons interact with search boxes and realize that those patrons with cognitive disabilities may be unable to form Boolean searches. Good user design invests in search engine processing, so users who need to use natural language in their search queries can get the same results as those who are able to form structured search queries.

REAL-LIFE SCENARIO

A library website wants to make its catalog searching be more user friendly. The librarian looked at recent search terms and found ones such as:

- Books by Robert Frost
- What time are you open?
- Pay my fine
- Audiobooks
- Shakespeare

She noticed that most of the search terms were not formally structured queries, but rather they were how people would naturally ask questions. She was able to propose that the library website run a search engine that could parse natural language questions like these and got rid of Boolean searches altogether.

Photosensitivity and Neurological Disorders

There is a category of disorders where people react negatively to lights, sounds, and movement on websites. The negative reactions can vary in type, length, and severity, depending on the neurological disorder. These reactions range from mild headaches to dizziness or vertigo, and from motion sickness to seizures.

Photosensitive Epilepsy

The most known and most commonly talked about disorder is photosensitive epilepsy. This is when flashes or flickers of lights and colors can cause seizures. What determines whether something causes a seizure is the hertz (Hz) of an item, or the number of times something happens in a second: the number of times a light flashes in a single second, or the color changes in a second, or how many times the website text refreshes itself in a second. Most people are sensitive to the 15–30 Hz range, but some people can be sensitive up to 3 Hz (Epilepsy.org 2015). If you have a web page that includes flashing graphics or videos with quick color changes, it can cause seizures if it happens more than three times a second.

There are ways to avoid this in the website design portion—by freezing video frames to ensure a light doesn't flash more than three times a second or slowing down animated graphics. People who have photosensitive epilepsy rely on content warnings, so if you know that a video, game, graphic, or other item on your website includes flashing lights, there should be a content warning. If you are unsure whether something on your website flashes, there are analysis tools available to download that analyze a website for flashes:

- The University of Maryland's PEAT, the Photosensitive Epilepsy Analysis Tool
- The Cambridge Research Systems Harding FPA

Assistive Technology for Photosensitive Epilepsy

Photosensitive epileptics can use some assistive technology if their epilepsy is severe enough that it impacts their quality of life. These assistive devices are generally non-technological but can radically reduce the risk of seizures by limiting light. This is typically done either by wearing an eye patch on one eye, which limits the amount of neurons that are triggered by light, or by wearing blue-tinted glasses, which limits light from the red spectrum (the most common seizure-inducing color).

Even though photosensitive epilepsy is rare, it can be life threatening and must be taken seriously. Flicker rates and spectrum analysis should be done on any website, both public and internal, as people do not always know that they have photosensitive epilepsy until after a seizure is triggered by something they see. The best practice is to analyze everything and place a content warning if you are unable to change the rate of flicker.

Key Points

This chapter talked about the ways that users process the information they find online and methods that you can use to ensure that the information is accessible to those with cognitive disabilities. Key points to remember:

- Keep the reading level at or below a ninth-grade level.
- Avoid library jargon.
- Write clearly and concisely.
- Keep the website easy to navigate with wayfinding markers.
- Avoid unnecessary distractions or flickering images.

Further Resources

Reading Level Analysis Tools

- Readable.io: https://readable.io/text/
- Hemingway: http://www.hemingwayapp.com/
- Microsoft Word: https://support.office.com/en-gb/article/Test-your-document-s-readability-85b4969e-e80a-4777-8dd3-f7fc3c8b3fd2

Photosensitive Epilepsy Analysis Tools

- PEAT: https://trace.umd.edu/peat
- Harding FPA: http://www.hardingfpa.co.uk/
- Online Flash Test: http://www.onlineflashtest.com/

Natural Language Processing Tools

- IBM Watson: https://console.ng.bluemix.net/catalog/?category=watson
- Stanford CoreNLP: https://stanfordnlp.github.io/CoreNLP/
- Natural Language Toolkit: http://www.nltk.org/

References

Alzheimer's Association. 2017. *Latest Facts & Figures Report.* Accessed May 18, 2017. https://www.alz.org/facts/overview.asp.

American Dyslexia Association. n.d. "About Dyslexia." Accessed May 18, 2017. http://www.american-dyslexia-association.com/Dyslexia.html.

Epilepsy.org. 2015. "Photosensitive Epilepsy." March 2015. https://www.epilepsy.org.uk/info/photosensitive-epilepsy.

McGraw, Harold. "SMOG Formula." Accessed May 14, 2017. http://library.med.utah.edu/Patient_Ed/workshop/handouts/smog_formula.pdf.

Moreno, Susan, and Carol O'Neal. 2000. "Tips for Teaching High-Functioning People with Autism." Indiana Resource Center for Autism. https://www.iidc.indiana.edu/pages/Tips-for-Teaching-High-Functioning-People-with-Autism.

National Center for Education Statistics. n.d. "Demographics—Overall." *National Assessment of Adult Literacy.* Accessed April 30, 2017. https://nces.ed.gov/naal/kf_demographics.asp.

Usability.gov. n.d. "User Interface Design Basics." Accessed June 1, 2017. https://www.usability.gov/what-and-why/user-interface-design.html.

CHAPTER 5

Motor Disabilities and Assistive Technology

IN THIS CHAPTER

- ▷ A range of motor disabilities, from arthritis to full paralysis
- ▷ The issues people with motor disabilities encounter when accessing websites
- ▷ Assistive technology for motor disabilities, including foot switches, head wands, and eye-tracking devices

ACCORDING TO STATISTICS, NEARLY ONE IN EIGHT American adults report some form of motor or mobility disability (CDC 2015). The disabilities can range in severity and form from complete paralysis to limited exertion fatigue. When it comes to accessing websites, most people think of Stephen Hawking or people who are unable to move their arms to use a mouse or a keyboard. While these people do epitomize those with motor disabilities, all forms of disability are ranges within which people fall.

Motor disabilities fall into some basic categories, each with its own specialized assistive technology. This chapter will cover some of the common disabilities that affect people's gross and fine motor skills, give examples of each, and explain the assistive technology available for use. Three common categories of physical motor disabilities that affect computer use are:

- Little to no use of hands or fingers: quadriplegia or amputations
- Tremors in hands and fingers: Parkinson's disease, Tourette's, or cerebral palsy
- Strain or fatigue: carpal tunnel syndrome, arthritis, or Ehlers-Danlos syndrome

Little to No Use of Hands or Fingers

When people think about physical disabilities and computer use, they usually think of people who cannot move their hands or arms. The most severe forms are those people who cannot move their arms, hands, or fingers, or have had them amputated. For people with these disabilities, it can be challenging to navigate websites as they often cannot manipulate a mouse or a keyboard. There are assistive technologies made expressly for this purpose, and which item one chooses to use will depend upon one's type and severity of disability.

Small Movement Assistive Technologies

Some of the assistive technologies for those with motor disabilities allow for a limited range of movement, such as finger twitches or using an elbow if a hand was amputated. Some of these technologies can be mounted on wheelchairs, to make the computer screen or controls easier to see, and some are mobile and can be used anywhere.

Switches

Switches are a category of assistive technologies that send binary commands to the computer (such as basic yes/no or on/off commands). Single switches can often look like a big red button, and if users can twitch their fingers they can use the button to navigate their computer. Some switches are more like switchboards that offer an array of buttons that each do different things: directional buttons for movement, a select button, and so forth. Which device individuals use, again, depends on their degree of disability.

When designing for accessibility, it is important to note that switches and other navigational assistive technology work with the same functions as a keyboard. Thus, if your website is keyboard navigable, it should be navigable by any of these other assistive technologies.

Foot Switches

If a user has use of her feet but is unable to use her hands, she can use a foot switch to navigate websites. Foot switches are a specialized slipper that users can wear to interact with a switchboard they place by their feet. There is typically a scrolling wheel and a number of buttons. Users can then control the computer by lightly stepping down on the different buttons or using the horizontal wheel to scroll around on the computer (TeachICT n.d.).

For users with limited foot mobility, there are single-button foot switches that only have one large button. Like regular computer switches, this single-button foot switch allows the user to navigate the computer or a website via a yes/no binary code. In addition to the single-button foot switches, there are switches with two pedals (one for each foot) where one pedal controls the mouse movement and one controls the mouse click.

Joystick Switches

Users who have even a tiny bit of mobility in their hands or fingers can often use joystick switches to navigate computers. These look similar to video game joysticks or a pen in a stand. The stick part navigates around the computer page (with a small push in each direction) and buttons on the stick itself simulate mouse clicks. Joystick switches are touch sensitive so they do not require much pressure to activate.

Head Switches

Users who have no finger use at all can use a switch with another part of their body that they can move. Switch buttons are often placed next to someone's head, so a quick sideways tap of the head will be able to move the cursor and navigate the website. Remember that switches (regardless of whether they are joystick switches or foot switches) take the place of a mouse and keyboard. If your website is fully keyboard navigable, it should also be navigable with switches and joysticks.

No Movement Assistive Technologies

If individuals have absolutely no range of movement in the hands, fingers, or feet, they require alternative methods of accessing and navigating websites. There are many forms of technologies that assist people with physical disabilities, and which technology they use, again, depends on the type and severity of disability.

Touch Devices

There is a class of assistive technology items that require some sort of touch from the mouth or the head. These technologies take the place of a keyboard and mouse and help the user navigate computers and websites.

Head Wands

A head wand is a piece of headgear (worn like a headband) that has a repositionable wand coming off from the forehead. Users who have no movement in their hands or feet but are able to move their head can use the wand to tap on individual keys on a regular keyboard or an adaptive keyboard. Keyboards that are meant to work with wands are incredibly touch sensitive, so users don't have to put much pressure at all to get the key to register their tap.

Mouth Sticks

Much like head wands, mouth sticks are a type of stylus, or pointing device, that a disabled person can use to click keys on a regular or adaptive keyboard. The mouth stick is a repositionable long wand with a silicone mouth guard at the end of it, to fit around the users' teeth for comfort. Because the mouth guard fits around their teeth, mouth sticks do not require users to clench their teeth tightly or hold anything between their lips. The wand is attached to their teeth, and they are able to point and select keys on the keyboard.

Sip-and-Puff

A "sip-and-puff" is an assistive technology that relays commands to a computer based on whether a user breathes in (sips) or breathes out (puffs). The small tube can either be attached to an earpiece (similar to a wireless microphone) or to a clamp that can be placed on a wheelchair or elsewhere. The tube connects to a small electronic device that measures the pressure within the tube and converts it to an electrical switch.

There can be variations with sip-and-puff devices, as it depends on how much breath control the person is able to exert. Some devices are a simple binary switch—puff or sip.

Other devices allow for variations in length and pressure of puff to do different things (Origin Instruments, n.d.). One device uses a long, forceful puff to mean page scrolling, while another uses short sips to equal a mouse click. Sip-and-puff devices, while not as costly as other assistive technology, can still cost hundreds of dollars to purchase.

Non-Touch Devices

For people who have no movement or touch ability, there are assistive technologies that do not require touch in any way. These motion-sensitive tracking devices help users who have little to no movements at all.

Head Tracking

Head-tracking devices are a setup that includes a computer-mounted motion sensor and its compatible software. The motion sensor scans the user's face and is able to track its movement and where it is pointing. The software then turns that tracking into mouse movement on the computer screen. To move a mouse cursor to the right, the user would just have to move her head to the right accordingly.

Eye Tracking

Eye-tracking devices are typically found on the forefront of virtual reality, gaming technology, and usability studies, but most companies that develop and sell eye-tracking software for business purposes also have a version that is expressly created for assistive technology purposes as well. Similar to the head-tracking device, an eye-tracking device site atop the computer monitor scans and tracks where the user's eyes are pointed. The corresponding software turns that eye tracking into mouse cursor movement.

Strain, Tremors, or Fatigue

There is a large swathe of users that may have plenty of free-range movement in their hands and fingers, but they may not be able to have the fine motor control needed to click small keyboard buttons or to move a mouse cursor to a tiny checkbox on a website. Some of these users have severe disorders, like Parkinson's disease, Tourette's syndrome, or cerebral palsy where they do not have complete neurological control over the movements of their arms, hands, or fingers. Other users who have disorders like carpal tunnel syndrome, arthritis, or Ehlers-Danlos syndrome may be able to fully control their movements, but suffer from muscle strain or fatigue. There are assistive technologies for both of these groups of users.

Lack of Muscle Control

If a user's hand shakes, jerks, or trembles, it can be very hard to accurately control a regular mouse or type on a typical keyboard. Both of these tasks require a level of fine motor control that is usually not seen in users with a lack of muscle control. While these users can use assistive technology that offers bigger buttons and tracking balls, website designers can design websites to be more accessible to this portion of users as well.

For users with a lack of muscle control, the assistive technology is intended to negate the spasms and tremors in a hand. There are mouse devices that require a sustained pressure to move, so small twitches will not move the mouse. There are keyboards that offer a larger surface area for the keys, so you don't need to be as precise.

Assistive Technology for Hand Tremors

In addition to external devices, most operating systems come with accessibility options built into the preferences of the OS itself. These accessibility options allow the user to completely customize how the keyboard and mouse control the screen:

- Sticky keys
- Filter keys
- Click-lock
- Double-click

Sticky Keys

Sticky keys is a setting that makes functional keys (such as the Control key or the Shift key) "sticky" in that the user does not need to hold them down to use that function. If you want to type a capital letter, you need two fingers: one to hold down the Shift key and one to type the letter. Sticky keys makes it so that once you hit the Shift key and let go, it is still active until you click the key again. This way a user with less manual control is able to press the Shift key, press the letter, then press the Shift key again to turn it off.

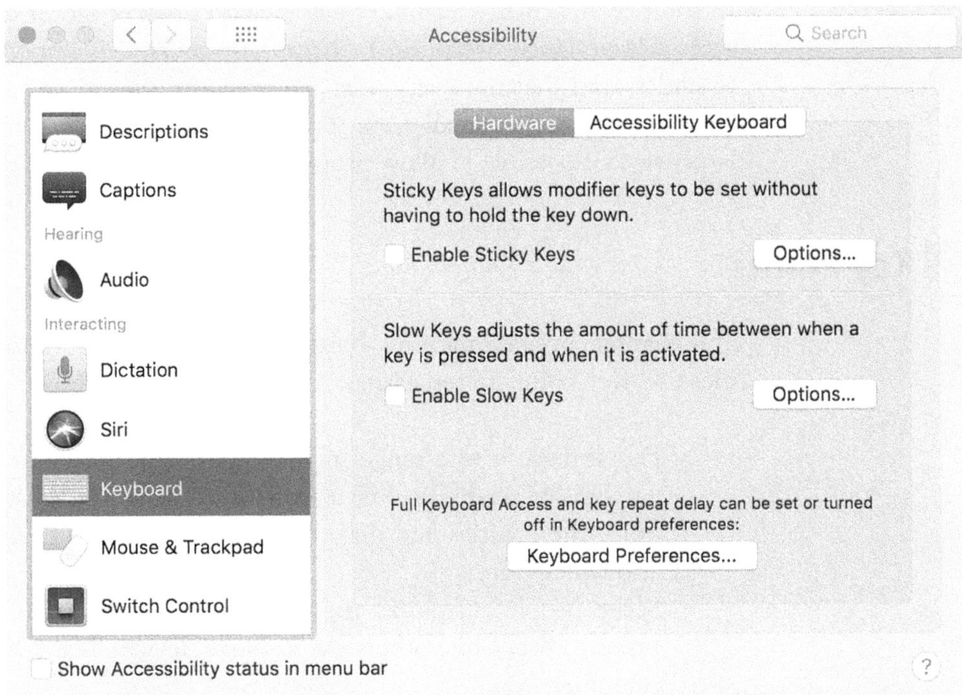

Figure 5.1. Mac OSX keyboard accessibility settings, including sticky keys

Filter Keys

Filter keys is a setting that tells the computer to ignore repeated keystrokes within a set period of time. By default, if you press and hold a letter key for a second, you will see that letter repeated a few times on your screen. People with less motor control typically press harder and need more time to complete a single keystroke. When those users turn filter keys on, they can tell the computer that any key that is held down for up to two seconds should only count for one click. This gives the user more time to complete a single keystroke.

Click-Lock

When a user wants to drag something on the screen or highlight a portion of text, he needs to press down on the left mouse button and hold it while he moves the mouse. Many users with a lack of motor control are unable to hold the button down for the period of time required to move an item or highlight text. Click-lock tells the computer that when a user clicks the mouse, it is the start of a drag event, and the drag event doesn't end until the user clicks the mouse a second time.

Double-Click

There are many times that a user will need to double-click on an item to activate or download it. If a user has tremors in her hand, it is very difficult to double-click with the speed needed to count as a double-click, instead of two single clicks. Users can change the speed in which their two clicks are seen as a double-click to whatever speed is comfortable for them. That way, they can single-click and double-click at their own speed.

Website Design for Hand Tremors

In addition to assistive technology, users with a loss of motor control benefit greatly from accessible design in websites. To help these users, it is important for website designers to understand that not every user can pinpoint a small area on the screen. If you have checkboxes or other small areas that require a mouse click to activate, be sure to offer larger sizes if possible to allow people more room for errors.

Key Points

This chapter covered motor disabilities and the assistive technologies people with disabilities use. Key points to remember:

- People have a vast range of muscle and motor control, ranging from complete paralysis or cerebral palsy to arthritis or carpal tunnel syndrome.
- Since the abilities and diagnoses vary so much, the individual technology needs also widely vary.
- Some people customize the computer itself to make the keyboard and mouse easier to use, while others use assistive devices, like a head wand, to navigate the computer.
- It is possible to design a website for people with motor disabilities if you design for the least mobile first.

References

CDC (Centers for Disease Control and Prevention). 2015. "Key Findings: Prevalence of Disability and Disability Type among Adults, United States—2013." Disability and Health. August 20, 2015. https://www.cdc.gov/ncbddd/disabilityandhealth/features/key-findings-community-prevalence.html.

Origin Instruments. n.d. "Sip and Puff Switch Solutions." Accessed April 29, 2017. http://www.orin.com/.

TeachICT. n.d. "Foot Control." Accessed May 20, 2017. http://www.teach-ict.com/gcse_new/computer%20systems/disability_accessibility/miniweb/pg3.htm.

CHAPTER 6

The Digital Divide

IN THIS CHAPTER

- ▷ The history of the digital divide
- ▷ Types of social disabilities
- ▷ The modern knowledge economy
- ▷ How to make websites accessible for people with social disabilities

The Digital Divide

IF YOU ARE SITTING IN A LIBRARY, COLLEGE, or almost any other place in the modernized world, it is easy to take internet access for granted. If computers are so affordable and basic internet is everywhere, surely everyone should have easy access to online information. This mind-set is a reflection of your place and privilege in the world. If someone considers internet access something that everyone could easily have, that person has typically never been poor, under-privileged, disabled, or rural. If one has ever been in one of these social categories, one knows that internet is not always easy to access. This chapter looks at each of these so-called social disabilities to understand what issues people face and how we can make websites more accessible for all.

Libraries and other educational institutions often put a lot of money and time into perfecting their mobile applications. Sometimes a library's mobile presence eclipses its real-world presence, from social media to QR code scavenger hunts. Putting so much effort into engaging those with immediate access to smartphones and the internet automatically ignores a large portion of patrons. The Pew Research Center (2016) put out a study on mobile phone ownership and found that smartphone ownership varies according to one's income, age, education level, and geography. In general, patrons are less likely to own a smartphone if they:

- Are sixty-five years or older
- Did not graduate from high school
- Make less than $30,000 per year
- Live in a rural area

By assuming that patrons have the ability for immediate internet access wherever they are, libraries ignore up to half of their patrons. The digital divide is a metaphor explaining that the privileged half of the world has easy internet access while the other half does not.

Poverty

In the United States, low-cost or subsidized broadband is ubiquitous. Ninety percent of families living below the federal poverty line have some kind of home internet connection (Digital Equity for Learning 2016). The problem is not that they can't get online at all, but rather they are under-connected or negatively impacted because of their poverty.

Poverty impacts internet access in many different ways, and not all are immediately visible. People living below the federal poverty line may struggle with slow internet speeds. They may live in neighborhoods that still rely on dial-up internet or in densely populated apartments where all residents share cables or hardware. A family may share one computer between all family members, so internet time is strictly allocated by urgency and need, as opposed to a leisure activity. People in poverty may fall behind on their bills and their connection is intermittently disconnected until they pay their internet bill.

All of these add up to an internet insecurity where people technically have access to the internet, but not always, and not on any predetermined schedule. Much like food insecurity, where people are not sure where their next meal will be coming from, internet insecurity means that they do not know if they will be able to get online at any specific time. Businesses and libraries who move fundamental tasks to online-only (such as renewing loans or paying fines) make these basic tasks difficult for people who are unsure if they will be able to access the internet when they need to.

Age

It should be no surprise that the older a person is, the less likely that person is to own cutting-edge technology. Research has shown time and again that elderly people are slower to adopt new technology and often prefer to complete tasks the way they are comfortable doing it. Elderly people are more likely to physically come into the library to ask reference questions (instead of searching for something on Google). Partially this can be because it's the way they remember libraries working in the past—they may get frustrated with the online catalog and wax lyrical about the virtues of the old card catalogs. While the rate is changing, elderly people often tend to live on the other side of the digital divide and prefer to do things in person, if at all possible.

In addition to their slow emerging technology adoption rate, elderly people are often sick or disabled. They often have vision, hearing, or cognitive issues, so libraries that focus on website accessibility for all disabled patrons also help their elderly patrons.

Under-privileged

There are many people who fall into a general category of "under-privileged," which means that they do not have the same standard of living or privileges as most members of society. This can include those in poverty but is a broader category than strictly economic. It can also include a lower level of education (e.g., high school graduate or less), living paycheck to paycheck, holding entry-level jobs, and so forth. Under-privileged people cannot be expected to have the same access to internet as the majority of the population.

If internet access is seen as a standard of living, under-privileged people often do not have the time, money, or knowledge to keep consistent internet access. People who live in under-privileged areas or conditions may not own their computer but instead may rely on gaining internet access from public spaces, like libraries or community centers.

Rural Geography

When thinking about users' ability to access the internet, you don't often think about where they live as a factor. Even in a modern country like the United States, however, there are broad swathes of rural land that still rely on antiquated dial-up internet. This is often due to remote locations, distances from urban centers, or low populations. Just like some places are so rural as to be reliant upon generators instead of electricity, there are places where fast internet has not penetrated.

People who live in rural areas like this, much like other under-privileged people, often rely on community centers or public libraries for reliable internet. Rural areas also have less cell phone coverage, so there are fewer opportunities to gain access to the internet.

The Knowledge Economy

A knowledge economy is when information and knowledge are commoditized and turned into something of value. This happens when the bulk of work shifts more to cognitive skills as opposed to manual labor—the new core competencies in the workforce are knowledge and information management (Shahrazad 2017, 216). What this means, then, is that access to information is now a vital part for functioning successfully in society. If a broad group of people are unable to access information, then they are unable to be a fully functioning member of society. Website accessibility is now not just something that is nice to have, but is imperative to have for the well-being of patrons.

Data, Information, and Knowledge

It is easy for people who have never been in a socially under-privileged situation to scoff at the thought of something like this called a "disability," but people who are unable to access information online for any of these social reasons often are unable to participate in modern society as they should.

Data itself is just the raw numbers, letters, and words that collect together in different places for different reasons. For instance, if I were collecting data on library catalog usage, my data would just be a set of numbers and words. Information is giving that raw data structure and organization, which then also gives it meaning and context. It orders the numbers and words into a specific data set and series, with labels and titles that explain what the numbers are. Knowledge is taking that information and using it to make decisions and predictions.

When under-privileged people are unable to access data or information online, then they are denied that opportunity to form knowledge about that particular subject. That denial of knowledge is a societal disability.

Knowledge Workers

If there is an entire set of under-privileged people who are denied the ability to access data and information online and thus form knowledge, how are those same people expected to participate in the current knowledge economy? Employees are more valued now for what they know and how they can apply it instead of their degrees or awards. If you look at open job positions, many positions are information positions—that of doing something with knowledge. This can include IT help, project management, customer support. These typical departments don't actually make anything physical—their entire value is in the knowledge the team brings to the company.

If society is denying an entire group of people access to information, then it is the library's mandate to step up and stand in the gap for free internet and knowledge education. There are no assistive technologies for a societal disability like poverty or age. The only assistance is civic—a personal one-to-one connection with the library as a lynchpin of the community.

Website Accessibility for Social Disabilities

There are some considerations to keep in mind when creating websites for people with social disabilities. The most important one is that they will likely be internet insecure—meaning that they will not have a reliable internet connection. It may be really slow or they may not always have access to it. There are a few things you can do for these two scenarios.

Slow Internet

If patrons have slow internet, their browsers may often display websites without style sheets or images. While this typically results in a poor user experience, if the web designer can design a website with a good no-style-sheet fallback in mind, then even a bad connection can still equate to a good experience.

Designing for no style sheets requires the use of specialized browser plug-ins or software that can turn off styles on your browser so you can see what a website would look like to someone with a slow internet connection. You can see if the structure makes sense at first glance, if it is organized, or if the point of the page is obvious. It will also become clear whether you've filled out alternative image tags, and you can see whether your image titles make sense given the layout of the page. In a slow internet context, you must experience it to design for it.

Unreliable Access to the Internet

It is an expression of privilege to assume that all library patrons have access to an internet connection whenever they need to. With the all too common mass migration to electronic resources, as opposed to print resources, libraries are effectively saying that if you want to use our services, you must be connected to the internet. This cuts off a small portion of users who do not know when they will be able to access the internet.

For those users, it is very important to promote non-internet options. If there is an internet sign-up sheet for an after-school coding class, make sure that the class is advertised at schools and that you allow kids to come in to sign up at the desk or to call in. Essential services, like fine payments and book renewals, should always be available in a non-online format as well as an online format, to help those people on the other side of the digital divide.

Key Points

This chapter covered the very basics of the digital divide and the foundations of social disabilities. Key points to remember:

- The digital divide is real and means that there are places with little to no access to the internet.
- Some social and economic reasons that someone might not have easy access to the internet are poverty, rural geography, and age.
- In today's knowledge economy, with so much data and information solely online, it is incumbent upon the library to step into the gap to provide any missing internet access.

References

Digital Equity for Learning. 2016. http://digitalequityforlearning.org/.

Pew Research Center. 2016. "Demographics of Mobile Device Ownership and Adoption in the United States." http://www.pewinternet.org/fact-sheet/mobile/.

Shahrazad, Hadad. 2017. "Knowledge Economy: Characteristics and Dimensions." *Management Dynamics in the Knowledge Economy* 5 (2): 203–25.

CHAPTER 7

Laws, Organizations, and Standards

IN THIS CHAPTER

- ▷ The legal foundation of accessibility
- ▷ Current laws and regulations
- ▷ Web accessibility standards

The Legal Basis for Accessibility

THE PRIMARY RATIONALE THAT ORGANIZATIONS GIVE when asked about accessibility accommodation is that the law requires them to. That is a valid reason, if somewhat simplistic, for any accessibility change. This chapter will give a brief look at the laws that cover disability accommodation and unpack what that means for libraries.

While it recaps the laws that govern access for people with disabilities, this book is not a legal book and does not give any legal advice. It will look at these laws through the lens of web accessibility for libraries. It will also cover the non-governmental organizations (NGOs) that help to codify what accessibility accommodation means in websites and technology. While these NGOs do not have the legal standing a federal statute does, they nonetheless set the standards and inform those very same laws.

Current Laws and Regulations

There are some foundational laws in the United States that relate to the rights of people with disabilities, and there are numerous amendments and smaller statutes that cover very granular aspects of accessibility. This section will focus on the three biggest and most comprehensive regulations in the United States: the Rehabilitation Act of 1973 and its 2008 amendment, Section 508 (of the Rehabilitation Act) and its forthcoming 2017–2018 update, and the Americans with Disabilities Act of 1990, with its 2016 amendments. These laws cover vast swathes of ground, from the size of the aisles in the supermarket to what accommodations a disabled worker can legally ask for at work. Each of these laws came into being at different times throughout the past fifty years, and each is a product of their time and context and needs continual updating to stay applicable. The subsequent laws each build on and reference the previous ones to create a corpus, or body of work, to ensure that the rights and needs of people with disabilities are met.

The Rehabilitation Act of 1973

The original Rehabilitation Act of 1973 may seem biased and narrow in scope when looked at from today, but it broke ground when it was introduced in the 1970s. This act prohibited disability discrimination in the workplace, created federal committees for disability rights advocacy, prohibited discrimination in federal hiring practices, and required compliance from any federal program or subsidiary (United States Legal Code 2008). The sheer impact of this act should be noted by the fact that it is still in effect, just with several amendments and modernizations in place, which are addressed below.

Amendments to the Rehabilitation Act of 1973

The Rehabilitation Act was amended in 2008 to broaden the definition of disability to match what was in the Americans with Disabilities Act of 1990. The government had found that the courts were citing the Rehabilitation Act of 1973 as the reason why a person didn't fit the criteria for being "disabled" (ADA Amendments Act 2008) and thus were finding in favor of the employer. Considering the leaps and bounds that modern medicine and psychology has made in defining and uncovering new and existing disabilities, it is logical that the definition of "disabled" should periodically be updated in parallel.

Section 508

As recipients of government funds, libraries are particularly cognizant of the need for Section 508 compliance, but understanding how it fits into the broader landscape of disability law is vital in advocating for accessible websites in libraries. It's important to realize that it's not simply a stand-alone law, but part of a greater statute about the rights of people with disabilities to live, work, and play in a world that was originally designed to exclude them. Libraries are vital to living, working, and playing, and as such must keep their online information accessible to patrons with disabilities.

Amendments to Section 508

The U.S. government recently revised Section 508 again to keep up with the rate of technology. This revision was written in January of 2017 with compliance expected in 2018, but

THE REHABILITATION ACT (1973)

- Prohibited discrimination in the workplace
- Revamped federal hiring practices and committees
- Required compliance by institutions that receive federal funds

SECTION 508, REVISED 2017

- Grouped ICT by function, rather than by type of product
- Required WCAG 2.0 A or AA accessibility compliance
- Clarified that all forms of public-facing content and nine types of internal-facing content must be accessible

includes a "safe haven" umbrella for previously compliant websites (U.S. Legal Code 42). The new Section 508 restructures the Internet and Computer Technology (ICT) section by function, rather than by product. This move was a reaction to the pace of technological change because many modern ICT products fulfill many different functions—software that acts like hardware and hardware that includes software.

For example, the modern-day smartphone is an internet browser, telephone, video camera, still camera, and microphone all in one. Under the previous Section 508 rules, the smartphone maker would have to look in a number of different places for conformance requirements, which increased the possibility of conflicting information. In the revised Section 508, any product that includes web-based content must conform to WCAG 2.0 standards.

The WCAG 2.0 standards offer basic guidelines for what constitutes accessibility in websites and are addressed later in this chapter. The 2017 revision also clarified some confusing terms and elements and extended the accessibility mandate to any public-facing content and nine types of internal-facing documents.

The new Section 508 rules impact libraries because they increase the accessibility compliance level not just for public-facing websites and documents, but also for internal ones. Documents or websites that librarians create for staff need to be just as accessible as the websites that librarians create for patrons.

The Americans with Disabilities Act of 1990

The Americans with Disabilities Act of 1990 (more commonly known by its acronym ADA) greatly expanded equal rights for people with disabilities. It impacted every public and private sphere, from national parks to medical technology, and from small businesses to emergency management response. Most librarians should have a basic knowledge of the ADA. The common question, "Is it ADA compliant?," refers to whether the item or service in question complies with the regulations set out in the Americans with Disabilities Act of 1990, with the amendments that were added in 2008.

THE AMERICANS WITH DISABILITIES ACT (1990)

- Prohibited discrimination in any state, local, or federal program
- Required accessibility in travel and transportation
- Expanded the definitions of public accommodation to include privately owned spaces

ADA AMENDMENTS ACT (ADAAA) (2008/2016)

- Expanded the definition of "disability" to include ADHD and other cognitive and language challenges
- Mandated that the term "disability" apply without extensive proof of disability
- Expanded the definition of a "public space" to include websites and online spaces

With the ADA in 1990, Congress set out to provide "a clear and comprehensive national mandate for the elimination of discrimination against individuals with disabilities" (U.S. Legal Code 42) with sweeping regulations for public spaces, transportation, state and local government facilities, and even commercial institutions.

Amendments to the ADA

It was thought at the time that no stone was left unturned and that this law touched every sphere of a disabled person's life, but a growing body of case law proved otherwise. In 2008 the ADA Amendments Act (U.S. Equal Employment Opportunity Commission 2008) expanded three key strictures in the ADA: it expanded the definition of "disability" to include ADHD and other cognitive issues, asked that it be applied without extensive proof of disability, and expanded the definition of a "public space."

Title III Challenges

By 2008, Title III of the ADA stated that "individuals with disabilities have full and equal enjoyment of the goods, services, facilities, privileges, advantages, and accommodations," but it didn't necessarily mention websites or online services. In the ever-growing body of case law, courts had begun to include websites as part and parcel of "goods and services."

One of the biggest challenges to the online portion of the ADAAA came via the open education software provider Open EdX, which hosted online courses at Harvard, MIT, and other institutions. The courts found that their online courses were not accessible. Even though Open EdX disagreed that online information was covered under the "goods and services" clause, they agreed to a four-year settlement in which they were to prove compliance with the ADAAA (U.S. Department of Justice 2015). Due to this perceived conflict, the Department of Justice re-opened the ADA for revision. These changes were codified in 2016 as an expansion to the 2008 ADAAA to include websites as a part of the accepted definition of "goods and services" (ADA Amendments Act 2016).

Accessibility Standards

This section covers the international and technologically neutral organizations that help set the standards referenced in the U.S. accessibility laws. It will also elucidate as to what, exactly, the standards cover and clarify the differing levels of compliance.

World Wide Web Consortium ("W3C")

The W3C is an international consortium that focuses on standards to "ensure the long-term growth of the web" (WCAG 2.0 Overview 2017). It combines member institutions, staff, and the public at large into working groups to create and set standards. W3C knows that the unfettered and often wild nature of the internet does not lend itself to long-term growth, and so develops and advocates for standards in how websites are created, displayed, and made accessible. The W3C has created one of the best-known accessibility standards, the Web Content Accessibility Guidelines (WCAG 2.0), which have recently been incorporated into U.S. accessibility law.

WCAG 2.0 (2008)

The WCAG 2.0 guidelines give twelve standards split across four different principles, with each standard resulting in three possible compliance levels. The sections below will explain the WCAG standards, principles, and compliance levels.

WCAG 2.0 Principles

The principles can be recalled with a handy mnemonic: POUR. According to WCAG 2.0, websites must be:

- Perceivable: Users can recognize the content and that cannot be invisible to all of their senses.
- Operable: Users can navigate and use the system, via a keyboard, mouse, or other means.
- Understandable: Users can comprehend the system and its contents.
- Robust: This refers to the extent that assistive technologies can interface with the system.

WCAG 2.0 Standards

Within each of the four principles, there are specific standards that websites must meet. The standards are noted below under each principle.

Perceivable:

- 1.1. Provide text alternatives for any non-text content so that it can be changed into other forms people need, such as large print, braille, speech, symbols or simpler language.
- 1.2. Provide alternatives for time-based media.
- 1.3. Create content that can be presented in different ways (for example simpler layout) without losing information or structure.
- 1.4. Make it easier for users to see and hear content including separating foreground from background.

Operable:

- 2.1. Make all functionality available from a keyboard.
- 2.2. Provide users enough time to read and use content.

- 2.3. Do not design content in a way that is known to cause seizures.
- 2.4. Provide ways to help users navigate, find content, and determine where they are.

Understandable:

- 3.1. Make text content readable and understandable.
- 3.2. Make Web pages appear and operate in predictable ways.
- 3.3. Help users avoid and correct mistakes.

Robust:

- 4.1. Maximize compatibility with current and future user agents, including assistive technologies.

WCAG 2.0 Conformance Levels

Websites can conform to the WCAG 2.0 standards at three different levels or it is not compliant at all. Section 508 in U.S. law says that websites must meet Level AA compliance of the WCAG 2.0 standards. To be considered compliant, a website must meet all the testing tasks for that particular level. The testing tasks of each level are given under each of the twelve standards.

The conformance levels are:

- Level A
- Level AA
- Level AAA

This chapter will not cover each of the individual testing tasks in detail. To read about each of the testing tasks in detail, WCAG provides a handy, interactive tool that gives multiple scenarios for each testing task; or, check out the accessibility testing spreadsheets in appendix A.

WCAG 2.0 Revisions

There is a current working draft of WCAG 2.1 standards, but it will go through several revision cycles before it is accepted and published. Since current laws and regulations now explicitly reply on being WCAG compliant, it is important for librarians to keep abreast of when the new WCAG revisions will be codified. The working document can be viewed online (WCAG 2.1, 2017), but be aware that it is a living document and can change at any moment.

WAI-ARIA

The Web Accessibility Initiative–Accessible Rich Internet Applications (WAI-ARIA) is a type of accessibility markup that ensures the more dynamic applications like widgets, drag and drop activities, or tooltip hovers are accessible (WAI-ARIA Authoring Practices 2016). This is done via a set of HTML labels and other tags that explain the different

REAL-LIFE SCENARIO

A librarian added a video to the library website to promote Banned Books Week. He later then had to conduct accessibility testing to ensure that the website was still WCAG 2.0 Level AA compliant. To test the page with the new video, he would follow these steps:

1. Start with the Perceivable principle
2. Start with Guideline 1.2, Time-Based Media
3. Under the guideline there are different success criteria for each compliance level. There are two different success criteria that he could meet to be considered Level AA compliant:
   a. Success Criterion 1.2.4 Captions (Live) (Level AA): Captions are provided for all live audio content in synchronized media.
   b. Success Criterion 1.2.5 Audio Description (Prerecorded) (Level AA): Audio description is provided for all prerecorded video content in synchronized media.
4. If he wanted to reach for Level AAA compliance, he could meet the AAA success criteria:
   a. Success Criterion 1.2.6 Sign Language (Prerecorded) (Level AAA): Sign language interpretation is provided for all prerecorded audio content in synchronized media.

states of an item. The attribute for a dropdown menu that is selected is different than one that isn't selected. These attributes give needed information to screen readers and other assistive technologies about how the user interacts with the content on the screen.

ARIA tags explain dynamic web applications, such as:

- Drag and drop
- Dropdown
- Checkboxes or radio buttons
- Tabs
- Accordions or sliders

If a website showed two navigation tabs and each tab contained different content, the screen reader would not know that the items were tabs or were even shown on different pages unless there was an ARIA attribute stating that it was a tab. Specific ARIA attribute tags will be covered more in depth in the latter section of the book, including HTML examples.

Key Points

This chapter covered the foundational laws and statutes that underpin disability rights in the United States. It also covered the basic website accessibility standards.

Laws to remember:

- The Rehabilitation Act of 1973 and its Section 508
- The Americans with Disabilities Act
- ADA Amendments Act

Standards to remember:

- WCAG 2.0
- WCAG 2.1 Working Document
- WAI-ARIA

Further Resources

Legal Statutes

- ADA: https://www.law.cornell.edu/uscode/text/42/chapter-126
- ADA Amendments Act: https://www.eeoc.gov/laws/statutes/adaaa.cfm
- Section 508: https://www.section508.gov/

Organizations and Standards

- W3C: w3c.org
- WCAG 2.0: https://www.w3.org/TR/2008/REC-WCAG20-20081211/
- WAI-ARIA: https://www.w3.org/TR/2014/REC-wai-aria-20140320/

References

"ADA Amendments Act." September 25, 2008. https://www.gpo.gov/fdsys/pkg/PLAW-110publ325/html/PLAW-110publ325.htm.

"ADA Amendments Act." August 11, 2016. https://federalregister.gov/documents/2016/08/11/2016-17417/amendment-of-americans-with-disabilities-act-title-ii-and-title-iii-regulations-to-implement-ada.

W3C. n.d. "Introduction to Web Accessibility." Accessed March 26, 2017. https://www.w3.org/WAI/intro/accessibility.php.

U.S. Department of Justice. 2010. "2010 ADA Regulations." *Information and Technical Assistance on the Americans with Disabilities Act*. https://www.ada.gov/2010_regs.htm.

———. 2015. "Justice Department Reaches Settlement with edX Inc." April 2. https://www.justice.gov/opa/pr/justice-department-reaches-settlement-edx-inc-provider-massive-open-online-courses-make-its.

U.S. Legal Code. 2008. "Equal Opportunity for Individuals with Disabilities," 42 U.S. Code, Chapter 126 (1990). https://www.law.cornell.edu/uscode/text/42/12101.

U.S. Equal Employment Opportunity Commission. 2008. "Americans with Disabilities Act Amendments Act of 2008." September 25, 2008. https://www.eeoc.gov/laws/statutes/adaaa.cfm.

W3C. "WAI-ARIA Authoring Practices 1.1." December 14, 2016. https://www.w3.org/TR/wai-aria-practices.

———. "Web Content Accessibility Guidelines (WCAG) 2.1." Accessed May 15, 2017. https://www.w3.org/TR/WCAG21.

CHAPTER 8

Writing Content with Accessibility in Mind

IN THIS CHAPTER

- ▷ The ethics and reasons behind accessibility
- ▷ The right to information and advocacy of the oppressed
- ▷ Universal design for learning

Why Accessibility Matters

BY THIS POINT IN THE BOOK, WE'VE COVERED the various reasons why people have trouble accessing information online and the tools they use to overcome those challenges. We've also given a very brief review of the legal laws and statutes that regulate disabled access to online information. Knowing why you have to do something is one thing, but actually feeling the need to do so, without external stimulus, is something entirely else. This section will give a foundational purpose for librarians and accessibility, as well as create an ethical framework around accessibility in library websites.

The American Library Association's Code of Ethics gives broad statements about how librarians should react and behave when faced with difficult situations. The ethical code works as a framework within which librarians can make ethical decisions, and it includes ideals like freedom of information, customer service, and a commitment to the public good. Behind the code of ethics, however, lie a broad swathe of ethical philosophies that are important to articulate. Is it really doing any good if you follow the code of ethics but don't understand why?

Ensuring accessibility in websites can be difficult. It requires that you put time, resources, and thought into a website that most people will never overtly notice. It is common to face opposition to accessibility initiatives, both from without your institution and from within, and it is important that you are able to articulate exactly your reasons for advocating for accessibility. This chapter aims to give you the ethical background that you can use when you run across opposition to an accessibility initiative.

Philosophy Background

It is not necessary to be a philosopher in order to hold a personal philosophy about what it means to be and act human. Your personal philosophy is built, however unconsciously, upon centuries of philosophical and ethical research. To fully articulate the need for accessible websites, it's important to understand the philosophical and ethical schools of thought that underpin people's actions. We will cover:

- Deontological ethics
- Responsibility ethics
- Dialogical ethics
- Care ethics

This section will give you a basic overview of ethics and different lenses through which you can look at accessibility initiatives to make sure that you're doing it for the right reasons.

Deontological (Rule-Based) Ethics

Deontology is adherence to a rule-based ethics. In deontology, what makes an action right is its adherence to a moral law, regardless of the consequences of said action (Alexander and Moore 2016). The moral law says that we should only do what is right, even if the consequences of said action are not good: the right always supersedes the good. So according to typical deontology, if the law says that we should give or deny someone access to library information, we need to comply with that regardless of the consequences or effects of the action. There is little room for intent, motivation, protest, or civil disobedience.

When most people think of accessibility, they think of it in a rather deontological way. They think of it in terms of obeying the law or a moral norm. They do what the laws say to do without considering the effects of their actions. Deontology is very self-oriented—you're focused on obeying the rules because the rules are good (Constantin 2014, 432). In that definition, there is nothing about self-sacrifice, the greater good, or benefiting others. This is problematic because librarianship is a service profession—charged with helping others. Holding an ethical viewpoint that elevates your own needs above those of others may lead you to make decisions that harm library patrons.

REAL-LIFE SCENARIO

Many public administration offices abide by deontological ethics, even if they don't explicitly say it. A public librarian abides by the ALA Code of Ethics as well as specific institutional, state, or federal regulations and codes of professional conduct. The public librarian can form and hold his own opinions, but he must abide by the ethics laid down for him while he is at work.

REAL-LIFE SCENARIO

A librarian notices that the aging Korean population in her community keeps asking for resources that the library doesn't have. In responsibility ethics, her moral compass is defined by how she responds to that need. Obviously she can ignore it, which is a complete denial of responsibility ethics. As she is in a position to respond to that need, perhaps she can add resources to the library collection, advocate for grants or special funding, or create community activities for them.

Responsibility Ethics

Responsibility ethics is a way of viewing actions and ethical dilemmas not as a problem of "what does the law say that I should do," but rather as an innate response to a situation. Being an ethically responsible person means that you respond when you see a need. But along with this conscious action, you need to have the knowledge to understand your possible options. If you don't have enough information about the situation, you may not know all the possible ways you can respond (Sher 2010, 204). Responsibility ethics requires that you continually learn more about the world and all its contexts so you have more response options the next time you're faced with an ethical choice.

Responsibility ethics is contextual (Brownstein and Saul 2016, 32)—meaning that no two situations are exactly the same. In the case of website accessibility, the librarians can see the need a disabled person has for their online information and can respond to that need, but the disabled person also has a response to that same need. How a person responds to a seen need defines his ethical views. Both people in this situation (the librarian and the disabled patron) have many options available to them in how they respond to the issue—responsibility ethics is responding to a situation for the benefit of the other person.

Dialogical Ethics

Dialogical ethics is viewing your relationship with other people as two ends of a dialogue. When one person speaks in a dialogue, the meaning is filtered through the immediate context and interpreted by the listener. That listener then responds to her interpretation of the original communication, which is then interpreted by the original person. Dialogical ethics views the questions of "What should I do" as both poles of the dialogue. Every action that someone else does, I interpret through my past experiences and I react. The other person then interprets my actions through her experience and reacts as she thinks she should.

The most important thing about dialogical ethics is to remember that actions are filtered and interpreted by someone in a specific time and context (Card 2002, 145). Just as context plays an important part in a verbal dialogue, context is an integral part of how we interpret and react in dialogical ethics. No two situations will be exactly the same because there are always different contextual interpretations in play. The vital ingredient in dialogical ethics is to try to understand the context for all points of view and then decide how to react.

REAL-LIFE SCENARIO

A blind patron is getting frustrated because his screen reader won't read the library catalog results. His past experience with official websites is that his complaint gets shunted off into the recycle bin most times. He knows from experience that the only way to be heard is to complain loudly. He emails a complaint straight to the library director and then calls to ensure they hear his complaint. The librarian who answers the call had just finished a lengthy reference question for a patron and has no knowledge of website or accessibility. She was taken aback by the patron's anger and got defensive in return. Both parties in this situation have to make a number of ethical decisions about how they should and will handle the issue. Both parties have past experiences and knowledge that causes their actions, which are then interpreted by the other party in light of their own experiences.

Creating an Ethic of Care

Care ethics is a field of philosophical moral study that believes caring about the needs of others is foundational to life. We can't live without care—babies, elderly, and ill people all require care (Barnes 2012, ch. 2). Care ethics rests upon the fact that we all require care at some point or another and all are in a position to give that care at one point also. It sees individuals as always within a contextual relationship with other people—sometimes providing for others and sometimes depending upon others.

The Republic of South Africa calls care ethics "Ubuntu," which is "the principle of caring for each other's well-being. . . . Ubuntu means that people are people through other people. It also acknowledges both the rights and the responsibilities of every citizen in promoting individual and societal well-being" (Republic of South Africa 1997, 12).

Care ethics realizes that ethics isn't something ideal and remote, but something that needs to be evaluated on a case-by-case basis, depending on what is best for the individuals involved. Caring for the best interest of others is at the core of "service professions" like public administration, government, librarianship, health care, social work, and so forth.

Most moral codes for technology and service professions remain a general list of dos and don'ts, such as intellectual copyright respect, affirmations of free speech, and so forth. This generally rigid ethical list does not allow for a contextual relationship between two

REAL-LIFE SCENARIO

A patron who has mobility issues called the library help desk to see how she could get a copy of a new book when she can't leave the house. The librarian who answered the call realized that he was in a position to care for someone in his community, so he spoke to the library supervisor to see if any policy was already in place for this situation. No policy existed yet, so this librarian wrote a draft of a delivery service policy for homebound patrons. The librarian took care of the patron's needs and ensured that other patrons who have the same mobility issues would also be taken care of.

people, much less allow for the additional interface of technology. As librarians in a service profession, care ethics means that even through the interface of technology, there still exist two people on either side of the website—one in need of help and one in a position to give it. That is what care ethics boils down to for librarians. If there is a need for help, we must try to care for that need as much as possible.

The Right to Access Information

As a part of a librarian ethic of care, one way that librarians can care for others is to help them access information easily and quickly. There are many patrons who are dependent upon technology to assist them in accessing online information. It is the librarian's moral and ethical task to ensure that those patrons can access the library's information using their own assistive technology. Not because the ALA Code of Ethics tells us to, or because the U.S. government says so, but because we have a duty of care to provide for our patrons.

All patrons have the same right to access information, regardless of disability or level of assistance needed. By ensuring that library websites are accessible, librarians are exercising their moral responsibility to care for those in their communities.

Advocacy for the Oppressed

One of the main facets of protecting the right to access information is that librarians are placed into a position of advocacy by default. As the "gatekeepers" of information, librarians have a unique view into the needs and challenges of their communities. Librarians need to engage in the multicultural context within their own communities to find out who needs help and what kind of help they need.

This drive for advocacy for marginalized groups goes beyond accessibility and into the political and cultural realm as well. The ALA website has a specialized advocacy portal (ALA, n.d.) that shines a light on specific issues that affect libraries. The following topics are just a few of the many topics in need of special advocacy:

- Access
- Copyright
- Equality, diversity, and inclusion
- Intellectual freedom
- Literacy
- Privacy

Information is, by nature, political. It can be a political tool or a weapon, and it is the responsibility of librarians to safeguard its access and ensure the access is open. A noted Brazilian educator and anti-oppression advocate, Paulo Freire, said in his best-known work, *The Pedagogy of Oppression*, that "to surmount the situation of oppression, people must first critically recognize its causes, so that through transforming action they create a new situation, one which makes possible the pursuit of a fuller humanity" (Freire 1996, 28).

To fully serve the under-represented populations among the community, librarians must look for the causes of oppression and work toward transformative action, so that a new social situation can be born. By conducting accessibility testing, advocating for accessible websites, and working with patrons who have trouble accessing online information, librarians can work to eliminate oppression one patron at a time. Freire (1996, 88) extends this ethic of care to its fullest extent—that it "requires an intense faith in humankind, faith in the power to make and remake, to create and recreate, faith in their vocation to be more fully human."

Universal Design for Learning

Universal design for learning (UDL) is a method of curriculum development that originated as an inclusive initiative—it takes evidence-based research about the brain and how people learn and turns it into a framework for designing learning items that gives all people an equal opportunity to learn (CAST n.d.).

Librarians are often in a position of designing learning objects—whether it is a simple subject guide on how to access online resources or a full curriculum on a specific subject. True website accessibility starts before the website is even created. For a website to be accessible, the content itself needs to be designed for accessibility. UDL gives a framework for designing curricula or learning content to be accessible and covers three main areas:

- Representation
- Action and expression
- Engagement

This section will cover the basics of those three areas and give examples of how they could be implemented within the library.

Principle 1: Representation

The first pillar of UDL is to provide multiple means of representation. People differ in how they perceive and comprehend information. If you only present an item in one specific representation form (e.g., a graphic, image, audio file), you are privileging one

REAL-LIFE SCENARIO

A librarian needs to create a guide to locating genealogical resources at the library for inclusion on the library website. This librarian knows about the principles of UDL, so he incorporates different means of representation while writing the content of the guide. To help visual learners, he created a photo PowerPoint with written text and images. For audio learners, he recorded a separate narration of the PowerPoint that users can listen to in conjunction with the PowerPoint, or by itself. For people who learn through doing, he created a sample research task that users can follow along with step by step on their own computers. By offering these three different means of representation, the librarian offers patrons the ability to customize their own learning experience in a way that works best for them.

REAL-LIFE SCENARIO

A librarian is tasked with modernizing the library website, and he decided to use a custom blog theme for a library news portal. He marketed the library blog and added a sticky post that would always stay at the top of the blog, asking patrons for feedback on the blog. He embedded a short Google Form because he knew that Google Forms was keyboard accessible. He also provided a Print button in case the patron wanted to print the form and bring it into the library, as well as including the library's mailing address and phone number. This way, there were four different actions that patrons could perform to express their opinions: complete the form, print it off and bring it in, mail it, or call them on the phone.

category of users while another category suffers. What this principle of UDL means is that you should present the same information multiple times in different ways, and ideally, give users options on how they want the content represented (National Center on Universal Design for Learning 2014).

Just as the previous chapters talked about the importance of giving alternative methods of accessing the same information, UDL suggests something similar. Websites are ideal for representing the same information in multiple methods rather easily and can be incorporated at the design stage. While you are creating content for a website or online learning object, consider how else you can represent a specific learning objective or item.

Principle 2: Action and Expression

To express something is to convey meaning or make something known (*Merriam-Webster* n.d.). In the second principle of UDL, to provide multiple means of expression relates to how users plan and perform actions. Users will express their knowledge differently, so offering a range of options for different tasks allows the user to choose the action he prefers (Adams 2009, 106).

Expression comes in many forms depending on the type of action expected from the user. In an academic setting, expression of knowledge would typically mean a test or exam. The actions expected for website users are different and also vary: the user might be expected to fill out and submit an online form, to use a search box, or to click on a button. Each of those actions require higher-level cognitive processes and planning (University of Vermont n.d.). If you have actions on your website that you expect your users to complete, you should offer options and alternatives to those expected actions. The most common alternative is to allow for an alternative to physical actions—like allowing keyboard navigation in addition to navigating via mouse, or putting an email address and a phone number on your Contact Us page.

Principle 3: Engagement

The third principle of universal design for learning relates to how people engage with information and what motivates them to learn and act. Providing multiple means of engagement is really a new way of saying, "There's something for everyone." People find

REAL-LIFE SCENARIO

A librarian in a public library was tasked with creating a summer book club that appealed to patrons between the ages of five and eighteen. Obviously children and youths would not be motivated by the same things, so she created a plan to provide children options. Within each reading level, she created three paths to completion of the book club that readers could choose from:

- Path 1: Readers get badges (either physical pins or social media badges) for each level of the club they complete. This will engage patrons who need immediate gratification for motivation.
- Path 2: Readers accumulate stamps or points for each book they read and at the end of the book club can turn in those points for a prize. This will engage patrons who need both immediate and delayed gratification (by choosing stamps or points).
- Path 3: Readers just get the book club materials and are allowed to complete it on their own time. This will engage patrons who are self-motivated and actively avoid competitive situations.

By allowing all children and youths options that appeal to different engagement and motivation theories, the librarian has crafted a program that can appeal to a range of patrons.

their motivation in various places and through different means. Motivation is a complex aspect of neuroscience and behavior and attempts to answer the question "Why do people do the things they do?" In general, motivation is a behavior that leads to a certain goal or reward. In UDL it is important to realize that goals and rewards are different for each person, as are the motivating behaviors that lead to those goals and rewards (Simpson and Balsam 2016, 4).

Engagement and motivation relate to library websites in a very direct way: Libraries want people to interact with their websites. They want people to use the online catalog or to pay a fine online. Those are goals. What libraries need now is something to engage the goal-oriented behaviors. If you want a patron to use the online catalog, how is it presented on the website? It is impossible to appeal to all people through a single medium or format, but perhaps including a video, image, or animation might help engage people with the "Search for a Book" section. Motivation and engagement depends on each person's individual situation, personal history, and preferences (which change all the time).

The best thing a website can do is to provide tasks with a range of challenge, relevance, authenticity, satisfaction/rewards, and design (Wegener 2006, 29). If you just provide a list of books in plain text for search results, that will only motivate certain patrons. Most users need more to engage their attention, so adding in book images, descriptions, or even book reviews can widen the appeal to different types of patrons.

UDL and Technology

In its original design, UDL was created for learning and instructional design. It is widely used in schools, academic classrooms, and workplace training modules. In today's online, global society, people learn on the go, in smaller chunks and from non-traditional places like Facebook, YouTube, or Twitter. It is time that library websites are regarded as learning platforms as well.

Starting the design for a library website with UDL in mind will ensure that you reach the widest group of patrons possible. UDL and accessibility are two sides of the same coin—one focused on how the content is presented and one focused on how users can access that same content. By including UDL in your website accessibility process, you are enhancing your website value for your most vulnerable and often overlooked patrons.

Key Concepts

This chapter covered the ethical and philosophical reasons why accessibility is important and some basics on universal design for learning as a means of writing content with accessibility in mind. Key concepts to remember:

- Deontological ethics: Doing something because the rules and laws tell you it's the right thing to do
- Responsibility ethics: Doing something because you can respond to a need
- Dialogical ethics: Doing something based upon your interpretation of the context
- Care ethics: Providing care for others in your community

Universal design for learning principles:

- Provide multiple means of representation and comprehension.
- Provide multiple means of action and expression.
- Provide multiple means of engagement and motivation.

Further Resources

Resources on Ethics

- *Stanford Encyclopedia of Philosophy*: https://plato.stanford.edu/contents.html
- Book: *The Ethics of Care and Empathy*, by Michael A. Slote
- Book: *Pedagogy of the Oppressed*, by Paulo Freire

Resources on Universal Design for Learning

- National Center on Universal Design for Learning: http://www.udlcenter.org
- CAST UDL Studio Tools: http://www.cast.org/our-work/learning-tools.html
- Universal Design for Learning Implementation and Research Network: http://udl-irn.org/

References

Adams, Mike. 2009. *Towards Inclusive Learning in Higher Education: Developing Curricula for Disabled Students.* New York: Routledge. https://www.vlebooks.com/vleweb/Product/Index/249468?page=0.

ALA (American Library Association). n.d. "Advocacy University." Accessed May 7, 2017. http://www.ala.org/advocacy/advocacy-university.

Alexander, Larry, and Michael Moore. 2016. "Deontological Ethics." In *The Stanford Encyclopedia of Philosophy*, edited by Edward N. Zalta, winter 2016. Metaphysics Research Lab, Stanford University. https://plato.stanford.edu/archives/win2016/entries/ethics-deontological/.

Barnes, Marian. 2012. *Care in Everyday Life: An Ethic of Care in Practice.* Bristol, UK: Policy Press. doi:10.1332/policypress/9781847428233.001.0001.

Brownstein, Michael, and Jennifer Saul, eds. 2016. *Implicit Bias and Philosophy, Volume 2: Moral Responsibility, Structural Injustice, and Ethics.* Oxford: Oxford University Press. doi:10.1093/acprof:oso/9780198766179.001.0001.

Card, Claudia. 2002. "Responsibility Ethics, Shared Understandings, and Moral Communities." *Hypatia* 17 (1): 141–55. doi:10.1111/j.1527-2001.2002.tb00684.x.

CAST. n.d. "About Universal Design for Learning." Accessed May 11, 2017. http://www.cast.org/our-work/about-udl.html#.WRSbVFXyuUl.

Constantin, Eugen. 2014. "Deontology in Public Administration." *Contemporary Readings in Law and Social Justice* no. 6, 432–36.

Freire, Paulo. 1996. *Pedagogy of the Oppressed.* Translated by Myra Bergman Ramos. 2nd rev ed. London: Penguin.

Merriam-Webster. n.d. S.v. "express." Accessed May 11, 2017. https://www.merriam-webster.com/dictionary/express.

National Center on Universal Design for Learning. 2014. "Principle I. Provide Multiple Means of Representation." Last updated March 7, 2014. Accessed May 7, 2017. http://www.udlcenter.org/aboutudl/udlguidelines/principle1.

Republic of South Africa. 1997. *White Paper for Social Welfare.* Department of Welfare. August 1997. Accessed April 16, 2017. http://www.gov.za/sites/www.gov.za/files/White_Paper_on_Social_Welfare_0.pdf.

Sher, George. 2010. "Responsibility and Practical Reason." In *Action, Ethics, and Responsibility*, edited by Joseph Keim Campbell, Michael O'Rourke, and Harry S. Silverstein, 203–18. Cambridge, MA: MIT Press. https://doi.org/10.7551/mitpress/9780262014731.003.0011.

Simpson, Eleanor H., and Peter D. Balsam. 2016. "The Behavioral Neuroscience of Motivation: An Overview of Concepts, Measures, and Translational Applications." In *Behavioral Neuroscience of Motivation*, 1–12. Cham, Switzerland: Springer International, 2016. doi:10.1007/7854_2015_402.

University of Vermont. n.d. "Guidelines and Principles: About UDL." Accessed April 4, 2017. https://www.uvm.edu/~cdci/universaldesign/?Page=about-udl/guidelines-principles.php&SM=about-udl/submenu.html.

Wegener, Debby. 2006. *Training Library Patrons the ADDIE Way.* New York: Elsevier, 2006.

CHAPTER 9

Building an Accessible Website

IN THIS CHAPTER

- ▷ HTML document and web page structure
- ▷ The basics of accessible HTML
- ▷ WAI-ARIA
- ▷ Interactive widgets, fonts, and scripts

BUILDING AN ACCESSIBLE WEBSITE is as much planning and knowledge as it is the actual coding. That is why the bulk of this book focuses on the planning and knowledge surrounding what it means for a website to be accessible and what you can do about it. However, one cannot forget the fact that there is obviously some web programming involved in building a website, and some of that programming relates directly to accessibility.

This chapter will not focus on teaching you the basics of HTML, but rather it will focus directly on the aspects of HTML that relate to accessibility. It will focus on the actual page (document) structure, specifics about HTML markup, including images, multimedia, and interactive items, as well as ARIA tags.

HTML

While this book is not a primer about how to create a website via HTML, this section will cover the most common HTML elements that affect a website's accessibility and give you examples of what you should do to make these HTML items accessible. This section will cover text and links, images, multimedia, interactive items, and forms.

Document Structure

How the page is structured has a great impact on assistive technology like screen readers. Since screen readers read what is on the web page very linearly, if the web page is not structurally sound or standardized, then the user will find it very difficult to navigate or understand. Document structure relates to both the page title and language information, but also how the page is broken up into sections: a header, navigation, main body, and footer. There should be nested "divs" and sub-sections to keep like content grouped together. There should be a logical path to proceed from the top of the web page to the bottom. If you are in a position to change the document structure of the web page, then these are important considerations to keep in mind.

Metadata

The metadata on the HTML page may seem unnecessary, but it contains valuable information for browsers and any assistive technology to understand how the page is written and if there are any specific scripts on the page.

If you use a third-party content management system for your web page, the metadata typically is automatically generated and you do not have to worry about it. If you write your pages from scratch, you will need to ensure that your metadata is accurate.

Page Divisions

If you write your website from scratch, you will need to ensure that your web page is logically organized and that it uses divisions that make sense. The page should start with a <header> section and end with a <footer>: what divisions you put in the middle are ways to organize the content to make it easier for assistive devices and users to understand.

The most common divisions are a "main content" division, which encompasses the entire body of the web page (minus the header and footer), navigation divisions, and individual paragraph or content divisions. The paragraph or content divisions are named divisions, so be sure to name the divisions something semantic, or relevant. If you can get away from using divisions and use, instead, classes for other paragraph or header tags, that is much easier for screen readers and tells the browser more about the meaning of the content than a simple <div> tag can. Two such examples are the "time" and "address" tags in HTML.

For example, using the HTML <time> tag within the regular markup of the document (even mid-sentence) turns a series of words and numbers into a machine-readable

CODE EXAMPLE:

```
<!DOCTYPE html>
<html lang="en" class="no-js">
<head>
    <meta charset="UTF-8">
    <meta name="viewport" content="width=device-width, initial-scale=1">
<title>Your Web Page Title Here</title>
```

EXAMPLE OF POOR STRUCTURE (ALL <DIV CLASS> TAGS)

```
<div class="about">
    <div class="title">All About Me!</div>
    <div class="date">Date of Birth: August 1, 1995</div>
    <div class="address">123 Sunnybrook Ln, Anytown, MA 02110</div>
</div>
```

EXAMPLE OF GOOD STRUCTURE (MEANINGFUL HTML TAGS)

```
<div class="about">
    <h3 class="title">All About Me!</h3>
    <p>Date of Birth: <time datetime="1995-08-01 01:00">August 1, 1995</
time>.</p>
    <address>123 Sunnybrook Ln, Anytown, MA 02110</address>
</div>
```

date and time unit (w3schools n.d., "HTML DOM Time Object"). The screen reader, then, instead of reading August 1, 1995, as "August one, one nine nine five" will instead read the date and time as it should be read.

The <address> tag tells the machine who the owner of the page, article, or entire website is. While you may not see any discernible difference between the good and bad examples if you put them both on a website, it makes your web page easier to read by the machines that help disabled users access the internet.

HTML Text

When you are writing a set of text in HTML, there are some specific connotations that you should keep in mind as the text relates to accessibility. While text itself is relatively accessible for all forms of assistive technology, there are actions you can take to make it even easier for users to understand the page content. Avoid using symbols that screen readers have trouble reading, like dashes or abbreviations. The screen reader would just read the symbols aloud, so instead of writing "8–9" it would be more accessible to write it as "8 to 9." Simple and small changes make a world of difference for the user trying to understand what the screen reader is saying. This section on HTML text will focus on when you might want to include screen-reader-only content and best practices for links.

Screen-Reader-Only Content

Sometimes it is appropriate to add in some text that is intended only for screen readers. This "screen-reader-only" text is only appropriate when you have something to tell the user that only applies to screen readers. This usually means instructional information that is obvious to sighted users but could be confusing when read by a screen reader (WebAIM 2014).

REAL-LIFE SCENARIO

Jenessa is creating a web page and has included breadcrumbs in her navigation to show the users where they are and how that page relates to the overall web page hierarchy. Her breadcrumbs look like this to sighted users:

Library Home → Online Resources → Audiobooks

Since the breadcrumbs are also links, it can confuse patrons who use screen readers because it may seem like these links came out of nowhere or that the screen reader has jumped back up to the navigational links. To avoid this confusion, Jenessa added in a small bit of screen-reader-only text to explain that these links are the breadcrumbs.

The most common way to make something invisible to sighted users but still read by screen readers is to use CSS to "position" the text off the visible screen. Web designers commonly use in-depth CSS classes to style and hide something from visible users, If you need a quick and easy way to make a segment of text only visible for screen readers, you can simply set the style of the item to a negative text indent (so the item would be visible but it's way off the screen). This can be shown as <text-indent: -10000px;>.

Links

Hyperlinks may seem rather straightforward, with just the URL and the text, but there are important considerations and best practices to keep in mind for accessibility. When creating links, you should consider both the URL and the text, as well as how the link looks and reacts to a keyboard focus.

Link URL

The URL that a link sends the users to is a simple process for non-disabled users, because they have the contextual information on the page to understand information about the link. It is obvious if the new URL will open in a new browser tab or the same window. Generally the URL of a link is simple for assistive technology also. The only time that you should be concerned is if the link is used as more of a placeholder and doesn't actually go anywhere.

These links typically are used as navigational items, or as a part of a JavaScript function. They may be styled to not even look like links, so the user won't click on them, but assistive technology like screen readers or keyboards do not have that context and will read out or focus on any link. The disabled user will then be confused when the link doesn't go anywhere.

Example of a link to nowhere: <a href="#" onclick="return false;">

In the example above, the web designer wanted to show that some text was a clickable item, but didn't want it to send the user anywhere. A better way to style the text would be to use a button instead; that way screen readers and keyboard-only users won't be confused when they get to a link that doesn't do anything.

Link Text

The text of a link is what the screen reader will read aloud to the user, so it is vitally important to make the link text relevant and context independent. Users with assistive technology often tab through links as a method of browsing a web page, so they won't necessarily hear the link within its surrounding context.

Poor link text can be as simple as using the actual URL as the link text. Unless the URL is something short and to the point (like a main site URL), it should never be used as the link text because they are not easily readable. URLs often contain symbols, numbers, and random letters that are tedious when read aloud.

Another method of using poor link text is using something that depends on the context to be understood. This is commonly used for phrases like "Click here." Not only is it redundant in a link text to tell the user to click, but it also is meaningless out of context of the rest of the sentence. If disabled users are browsing the page by tabbing to the different links, they would rather have a link text that tells them where the link actually goes.

Link Appearance

For sighted users, links typically are underlined or somehow visually different to tell the user that they are clickable items. If you use something other than an underline, you need to consider the effect it may have on disabled users who are used to seeing underlined items as links. Some designers choose stylish formatting, such as shadows, imaginary buttons with rounded corners, and other visual devices.

Styles like this do not matter to assistive devices like screen readers, which do not read what a link looks like, but it matters to everyone else and is just better use design. If you do change the link appearance, just be sure that the link has a non-color indicator, like a shadow or an underline or bolded text for color-blind users.

POOR LINK EXAMPLES

- Click <a href="www.apple.com">here to learn more about Apple.
- Go to <a href="https://itunes.apple.com/us/app/apple-store/id375380948?mt=8"> https://itunes.apple.com/us/app/apple-store/id375380948?mt=8 to find the Apple app.

BETTER LINK EXAMPLES

- Learn more about Apple on the <a href="www.apple.com">Apple website.
- Go to <a href="https://itunes.apple.com/us/app/apple-store/id375380948?mt=8">the iTunes store to find the Apple app.

Keyboard Focus

If a web designer styles the link to react in a specific way to a mouse hover-over, he needs to make sure that it also reacts to a keyboard focus in the same manner. Remember, not all users use a mouse to navigate a website, so it is important to design functions and scripts to react to both a mouse hover *and* a keyboard focus (WebAIM 2013). This can be done as simply as adding "a:focus" to any "a:hover" that you format in your CSS.

Images

Images deserve special consideration to accessibility when you are using them in a website because they are visual media. There are many ways to make an image accessible, so this section will focus on the easiest and most common methods of image accessibility: alternative text and image links.

Alternative Text

The alternative text for an image is the guide for those who cannot see the image. The text must explain what the image is and if there is any text on the image. Some images are purely decorative, like logos or curlicues, and as such can be provided with a "null" alternative text. This tells the screen reader to skip over the image as it isn't important to the content.

You may choose, however, to describe even decorative images because deciding which image is important or not should be the job of the disabled person, not yours. Your job is to make the images accessible to all users (disabled or not) and allow them to decide which images are important and which ones they can forget about.

When crafting an alternative text for an image, you need to consider what someone would need to know about the image for it to make sense within the wider context of the page. If it is simply decorative and serves no other purpose than visual aesthetics, you can provide a simple description or a "null" text. If the image provides information that is not readily apparent in the surrounding context (e.g., new text or ideas, or serves as a point of contrast or comparison), then you need to be sure that information is given in the alternative text.

Screen readers will always say "image" before an image, so it is unnecessary to add the word "image" into the alternative text. The duplication of a word could be confusing to patrons who are listening to a screen reader. You should also ensure that your description includes contextual information about the image: Is it a photo, a painted portrait, or a cartoon? Depending on the context, the differences in the visual medium can include

ALTERNATIVE TEXT EXAMPLES

- No image alt text: <img src="www.url.com"/>
- Poor image alt text: <img src=www.url.com alt="Image of Lincoln"/>
- Better image alt text: <img src="www.url.com alt="painted portrait of Abraham Lincoln sitting on a horse at Gettysburg"/>

important nuances about the page. The best practice for image alternative text is to be as specific as possible, without being redundant or unnecessary.

Image Links

When using images as hyperlinks, it is vital that your image alternative text is descriptive, as it will be used as the link text, informing users where it will take them. There are two main considerations when using images as links: (1) that the text is descriptive enough so the user knows what to expect, and (2) that the description is concise enough to be used as a link text.

It is a fine line between being descriptive and being verbose. Image alternative text doesn't necessarily have a word limit, but it should be kept to a reasonable length, especially when used as a link text. Remember, many users tab between the links as a form of browsing the website, so having an alt text that is too long will mean that the user tabs away from the link before the text is finished. Be as concise as possible and be sure to place the most important information first.

Multimedia

Multimedia deserves its own special category of accessibility considerations when creating websites because it is particularly inaccessible by nature. Much like images, multimedia files are primarily designed for a single sense: audio files are meant to be heard and video files are meant to be seen. Because of this, you absolutely must have accessibility options for both types of files or you cannot claim to have an accessible website.

Video Files

Unfortunately, most out-of-the-box video players are minimally accessible, if at all. This section will cover the most commonly used video players, like YouTube and Vimeo, and specialist video players created with accessibility in mind, and cover what to do when uploading videos on social media.

YouTube

YouTube has made great strides in its accessibility since the days when its video player was based on Macromedia Flash. Now it is HTML5 based and offers more accessibility options (YouTube 2015). You still must do some manual configuration and setup, though, so it's not fully out-of-the-box accessible. The most important items to set up are the closed captions and the transcript.

YouTube automatically sets up default captions. While this may seem like a good idea in theory, the artificial intelligence that creates the captions often misunderstands words and creates nonsense captions or, worse, offensive language. You must go into the captions for each video and create your own caption track that will override the automatic track. That way, you can ensure that the video adheres to caption best practices.

If you write your own caption file, YouTube will automatically turn that into an available times transcript. Transcripts are not easy to find in most YouTube videos, as they are automatically available only on the video's YouTube page. Users must click on a small More button below the video, then click on Transcript. If the video is embedded in another page, however, the Transcript button is not available and users must click through to the video's YouTube page to be able to see the transcripts.

If you embed YouTube videos on your page, it is best practice to embed a video transcript on your page, instead of forcing users to click through to the YouTube page just to view a transcript.

Vimeo

Much like YouTube, Vimeo offers captions on the videos, but you must create and upload the caption yourself. Vimeo does not offer an automatic caption option or even a caption editor like YouTube does. You must create the transcript in WebVTT or SRT format and upload it yourself (Vimeo n.d.).

As a secondary note, Vimeo does not offer any available transcript or option to download or upload one, and as such is not recommended at this time as an accessible video player.

Able Player

Able Player is an open source video player built for accessibility and usability. It offers many different configurations, depending on your need and level of accessibility compliance. The most basic Able Player configuration just includes closed captions, but it is easy to add a timed transcript. It also offers a configuration for you to still use YouTube videos, but replaces the regular YouTube video player with the Able Player video controls and features.

The most accessible configuration includes both closed captions and transcripts, but also includes a button that makes a sign language translation video pop up. If you create sign language translation videos, then Able Player is the video player that offers the best user experience and support for sign language.

American Foundation for the Blind Video Player

The American Foundation for the Blind (AFB) created its own video player and released it as available to the public (AFB n.d.). This video player uses easy to see and use buttons instead of small icons, which can be difficult to see. It includes obvious keyboard access instructions and requires that the video transcript be placed below the video as plain text.

While a much more accessible video player than Vimeo, the AFB player was designed for blind people, so some features for those with other disabilities are minimized. It is lacking a synchronized transcript, so users cannot jump around the video based on the script. It also lacks narration speed and volume control, which are integral parts of an accessible video player.

Audio Files

Audio files are meant to be heard, so it is important to ensure that deaf or hard-of-hearing users are able to understand the content via other channels. There are many different audio players, so this section will cover the most common players and offer suggestions as to the most accessible options.

HTML5 INACCESSIBLE AUDIO EXAMPLE

```
<audio controls>
<source src="audio-format1.ogg" type="audio/ogg">
<source src="audio-format2.mp3" type="audio/mpeg">
Your browser does not support the audio element.
</audio>
```

Many web programmers think that simply using the HTML5 <audio> tag is enough, but the audio and video tags have not been built with accessibility in mind. General consensus in the HTML5 working groups is to leave the accessibility concerns to individual developers, which, while nice in theory, leaves little room for non-technical website creators.

HTML5 Audio

Most websites rely on HTML5 to play audio, but without extra configuration, the HTML5 audio tag is not accessible. As is, it offers no options for captions or transcripts, much less a sign language translation option.

Many programmers suggest adding text tracks and captions using JavaScript functions (w3schools n.d., "HTML Audio/Video"), but this raises many more problems than it solves. JavaScript functions are highly technical, and as such are out of the question for many librarians. If it requires a high level of web scripting knowledge, it is unlikely to be widely used. JavaScript functions also depend on browser support. Not all browsers support all JavaScript functions, so even if you are able to add in a text track, it may still not be available to all users. Something that is not available to all users cannot be considered accessible.

Able Player

Able Player, as mentioned in the previous section, is a great media player for videos, but it also works really well in making audio files accessible. It offers many different configuration options for audio files, so users can control the audio speed and the captions, can rewind and fast-forward the track; Able Player even offers a timed-transcript option. Able Player allows you to offer users complete control over how they view and interact with the audio file, including offering a button for a sign language translation video that is synced to the audio file, so when you pause the main player, it also pauses the sign language translation video.

Able Player is available as open source technology, and includes robust installation guides and a large community of developers and supporters. While some technical knowledge is required to implement Able Player, it is not as technical as scripting JavaScript functions from scratch.

Interactive Items

This section will focus on the more interactive items that commonly are used on library web pages, including drag and drop items, buttons, tooltips, and accordions. These interactive items can make websites more engaging, but at the same time they remove a large swathe of users simply because those users cannot use or access the information contained in those items.

Drag and Drop

Drag and drop items are typically created in the jQuery scripting language and require extra scripting to ensure that they are accessible. The main concern with drag and drop interactions is to make sure users can complete the activity using keyboard navigation. Many drag and drop items require a mouse click to trigger the function, so it is important to add ARIA tags to ensure that the drag item will recognize a keyboard stroke the same as a mouse click. By default, no drag and drop function is accessible—it must be augmented before it can be used by keyboard navigation, much less any other assistive technology.

HTML5 includes a new attribute called "draggable" that can make any item (a div, an id, or whatever) able to be picked up by the cursor and dragged. Did you know that links and images are draggable by default? But being able to drop that item in a specific area of the page and have it either duplicate or actually move requires quite a bit of event handlers and scripting. You need to tell the browser what to do when users click on the item (which, in turn includes three different events—mouseover, mousedown, and mouseup), but also define what happens on "dragstart," "dragover," and "dragend" (w3schools, n.d., "HTML5 Drag and Drop"). In short, there are a lot of places for keyboard navigation to get overlooked or forgotten in a drag and drop activity.

The best practice is that if you must use a drag and drop interaction, test it extensively via keyboard navigation and any other assistive technology you can before calling it accessible.

WAI-ARIA Specification

The Web Accessibility Initiative–Accessible Rich Internet Applications suite (WAI-ARIA, or ARIA for short) is a set of specific tags meant for existing interactive functions to provide some extra information about those functions to keyboards, screen readers, and other assistive devices so those devices can use the interaction just like a mouse user could.

The ARIA tags are specific metadata consisting of a set of roles, statuses, and attributes that you can add to existing HTML code to make interactions more accessible. This section will cover the most common interactions and detail the ARIA tags needed: buttons, tabs, popups, and dropdown lists.

Buttons

To start thinking about which items might need an ARIA tag, you need to think through the mechanics of operating that specific interaction and notice what you do to make something change. A button is something you click on to make something else happen, but even that can be broken down into more discrete steps, depending on what the button is supposed to do.

To "click a button," you first need to consider if anything happens while the button is pressed (the mousedown event) and if anything separate happens when you release the button (the mouseup) event. If something happens only while you keep the button pressed down, then you will need to ensure the user knows that it requires a second click

BUTTON EXAMPLE

If you have a Print button, it is easy because the action only happens when the click is completed. A Print button with ARIA attribute could look something like this:

```
<div tabindex="0"
    role="button"
    id="action">
   Print Page
  </div>
```

to turn the button off—similar to a Mute button. ARIA has an "aria-pressed" attribute that tells your assistive technology that the button is pressed—on the mousedown event (or initial keystroke on a keyboard) it changes that status to "aria-pressed=true," and on the mouseup event or second keystroke it changes to "aria-pressed=false."

Tabs

Tabs are a common method of organizing a web page so as users click on different tabs, they see different content. While nice from a visual perspective, from the point of view of a screen reader or assistive technology, all the content from all of the tabs are on one single page. So if you use tabs to organize content, it is important to also use the ARIA tags associated with tabs so the screen reader knows that the content is organized by tabs into sections.

Tabs are a bit more complicated to make accessible than buttons, but ARIA provides all the needed structure and attribute roles needed. It may be easier to think of your set of tabs as a list, with each tab title as a list item, and the text on that page as the list content. ARIA roles start from the top of the list and work their way down into the content, explaining what is showing on the screen and what is hidden. Remember, only one tab can be shown at one time; there needs to be a script running that changes around which list item is shown as "expanded" depending on which tab the user clicked. Here are some common ARIA tab attributes:

- aria-tablist
- aria-tabpanel
- aria-expanded
- aria-hidden
- aria-selected

Popups and Modals

Popups and modals are small browser windows that appear usually by clicking a button. These small screens can be simple dialogue boxes, error messages, or extra website content. The biggest accessibility problem with these is that screen readers and assistive technology typically cannot read the content within the popup and so the user never even knows it is there, or perhaps the user will be unable to close the popup via keyboard. Fortunately, ARIA includes tags specific to modals and popups that assist screen readers in reading the content and navigating away from it.

To be recognized by screen readers, any popup or modal widget needs to have the "aria-haspopup" element associated with it. This tag tells the screen reader or browser that there is additional content included that will show up on a popup. Again, as with other content that may seem separate to visual users, the content of popups will seem to be just regular content to the screen reader. Along with the "haspopup" attribute, it is also important to include both the "hidden" and the "expanded" scripts to tell the screen reader when the popup should be visible and when it should not. If the popup is important information and requires a response from the user, like an alert dialogue box or an acceptance of browser cookie policy, then the either "aria-dialog" or "aria-alertdialog" should be used.

Common ARIA tags for popups and modals include:

- aria-haspopup
- aria-expanded
- aria-hidden
- aria-dialog
- aria-alertdialog

Dropdowns and Navbars

It is a common and accepted practice to use dropdown lists as main navigation sections on websites. This can prove an accessibility hardship, however, if the screen reader doesn't know how to interpret the dropdown list. Dropdown lists are further complicated when each item within the list has a separate sub-menu of links to choose from.

DROPDOWN EXAMPLE

If you use a dropdown navigation menu with menu items that each include individual sub-items (like Research → Genealogy, Newspaper archives, or Online resources) you will need to be sure to include both "aria-haspopup" and aria-label="submenu".

```
<nav role="navigation" aria-label="menu with dropdowns">
    <ul class="with-dropdowns">
        <li><a href="#">Home</li>
        <li>
            <a href="/about" aria-haspopup="true">Research
            <ul aria-hidden="true" aria-label="submenu">
                <li><a href="/research/#genealogy">Genealogy</li>
                <li><a href="/research/#newspaper-archives">Newspaper Archives</li>
                <li><a href="/research/#online-resources">Online Resources</li>
            </ul>
        </li>
```

For dropdown navigation lists with sub-menus, it is important to use ARIA tags to tell the screen reader or browser that the menu item contains a sub-menu; otherwise, it will automatically treat the menu item like a link and go to that page. In this case, it is important to use a specific ARIA label (aria-label="submenu") along with the "aria-haspopup" element, so it treats the sub-menu like a popup or modal.

Customizable Options

One of the fundamental maxims about website accessibility is that no two users will use a website the exact same way or have the same needs. That is why it is important to allow users as much choice as possible as to how they want to experience the website. The most common customizable options are:

- Font size (text larger or smaller)
- Color (foreground vs. background contrast)
- Style (no CSS)

Font Size

Since no two users have the same needs as to text size for readability, the most accessible method is to allow users to choose their own font size by giving font increase and decrease options. These options are most typically seen on e-readers like Kindles, but are useful for any web page that includes large amounts of text.

Customizable font sizes are often conveyed as a set of letters in different sizes. In the source code, each letter set acts as a trigger for a JavaScript or jQuery event. The script says that when this item is clicked (an onclick function) something will happen; in this case, the CSS file will change to reflect one of the pre-set font sizes. There are many different methods to let users know that they have the option of customizing the font size, but the most common are shown with either a plus or minus sign or shown in different font sizes:

- Aa- / Aa+
- Aa / Aa

Color

Giving users the ability to change either the font color, the background color, or some combination of both allows for discrepancies in visual acuity and color blindness. If you have red text on a black background, it will be impossible for color-blind users to read the text. Giving them options to change the text color and/or background color to something they find more readable is a big part of making your website accessible.

Letting users know that they have the option of customizing the colors can be difficult but most commonly is done by using the "Aa" text (like the font size buttons) with a background for each:

- Aa (black text on white background)
- Aa (white text on black background)
- Aa (brown text on gray background)

No Styles

A final customizable option is to give users the ability to completely turn off all styling for the website. This is most useful for users who rely on keyboard navigation and screen readers (which do not care about styles) as well as users who are on slower internet connections. If users are connecting via a slow internet connection, they likely just want to complete a specific task. Allowing them to turn off styles will make the website load much faster for them and allow them to complete their task much more quickly and efficiently.

This is commonly called "style switching" and can be used if there is a page or section on your website that does not conform to the WCAG 2.0 standards. In that case, you would provide a link that users would click on and it would either change something about the page or bring up a new page with accessible content (W3C 2016). While this may get you to legal compliance, it is poor user design and would best be served with an accessible website that works for everyone.

If you must add the option to turn off or change style sheets, you could use an onclick function that will disable the main style sheet and select a new one (if you are changing styles instead of disabling them). Be aware, however, that good user design requires the browser to remember users' previous style choices when they move to a new page on your website. This will likely require session cookies that will temporarily store users' choice of styles and will make it active during their entire browser session.

JavaScript

The most important thing to remember when using JavaScript to increase the interactivity of your website is to ensure that users can stay in control over the content of the page. JavaScript is often used for interactive widgets like image carousels and autoplay for multimedia, both of which are poor accessibility options for users. When using JavaScript, it is important to always put the needs of the user in the center of your website design process.

Image Carousels

Including an image carousel that changes the image at a certain interval is a common interactive widget for websites. Libraries often use this for marketing and promotional graphics, which saves space on the web page because you can have a number of different images rotate in a single spot on the page.

Image carousels have accessibility issues, though, that must be addressed before your website can be considered accessible. Carousels that change images force the user to only interact with the image that is showing. If a user wanted to see the other images, or he just missed an image, there must be controls that allow the user to page back and forth through the images at his own pace. Simple buttons or text links like "Next/Previous Image" would allow users to regain control over the pace that they consume the content.

Autoplay

JavaScript is commonly used to force a video or audio file to start playing as soon as a user accesses a page of a website. The accessibility issues inherent in this once again go back to confusion and a lack of control over the website contents.

If a user accesses a web page and something automatically starts playing on it, it causes confusion because it's often not immediately clear what is playing or making the noise. This confusion is compounded when the audio plays and drowns out what the screen reader is saying. This can negatively affect the user and is a poor user experience, in addition to being a non-accessible experience.

The most accessible choice is to give the user full control over when a multimedia item starts or stops. If you do not have a choice and something must play automatically, you must give the user clear controls to stop it immediately.

Key Points

This chapter covered the basics of HTML as well as WAI-ARIA best practices for accessibility. Key points to remember:

- Always use alternative image text.
- Your hyperlinks should make sense when read aloud.
- WAI-ARIA tags add context to intricate items like tab panes and dropdowns.
- The more customizable options you offer the user, the better the accessibility.

Further Resources

- HTML5 Feature by Browser: http://www.html5accessibility.com/
- ARIA Roles Cheat Sheet: http://karlgroves-sandbox.com/CheatSheets/ARIA-Cheatsheet.html
- Session Cookies: https://www.w3schools.com/js/js_cookies.asp

References

AFB (American Foundation for the Blind). n.d. "Accessible Video Player, Version 1.1." Accessed August 8, 2017. http://www.afb.org/info/programs-and-services/technology-evaluation/creating-accessible-websites/download-afbs-accessible-html5-video-player/1235.

Vimeo. n.d. "Captions and Subtitles." Help Center. Accessed August 8, 2017. https://help.vimeo.com/hc/en-us/articles/224968828-Captions-and-subtitles.

WebAIM. 2013. "Link Text and Appearance." Links and Hypertext. Last updated October 3, 2013. http://webaim.org/techniques/hypertext/link_text.

———. 2014. "CSS in Action—Invisible Content Just for Screen Reader Users." Last updated December 11, 2014. Accessed August 3, 2017. http://webaim.org/techniques/css/invisiblecontent/.

W3C. 2016. "Using a Style Switcher to Provide a Conforming Alternate Version." https://www.w3.org/TR/WCAG20-TECHS/C29.html.

w3schools. n.d. "HTML Audio/Video DOM Reference." Accessed August 8, 2017. https://www.w3schools.com/tags/ref_av_dom.asp.

———. n.d. "HTML DOM Time Object." Accessed August 3, 2017. https://www.w3schools.com/jsref/dom_obj_time.asp.

———. "HTML5 Drag and Drop." Accessed August 10, 2017. https://www.w3schools.com/html/html5_draganddrop.asp.

YouTube. 2015. "YouTube Now Defaults to HTML5 <video>." *YouTube Engineering and Developers Blog*. January 27, 2015. https://youtube-eng.googleblog.com/2015/01/youtube-now-defaults-to-html5_27.html.

CHAPTER 10

How to Conduct Accessibility Testing

IN THIS CHAPTER

- ▷ How to create an accessibility testing plan
- ▷ How to conduct accessibility testing, both manually and automated
- ▷ How to get people with disabilities involved in your accessibility testing

IF YOU WANT TO TEST YOUR LIBRARY WEBSITES for accessibility compliance, it can seem like a mammoth task when you first start out. After reading about the many different types of disabilities and assistive technologies that people use to overcome them, you may feel overwhelmed or like you can't possibly cover every aspect of accessibility. That is entirely true and a valid way to feel when starting any accessibility testing. It is impossible to ensure that your website will work for everyone in every single situation. Your task, as the accessibility tester, is to ensure that your website is accessible for the largest amount of people possible at the time of testing.

Before You Start

Before you start your accessibility testing, you must spend some time thinking about *what* you are doing and *why* you are doing it. Creating a rationale and a plan for your testing are the most important parts of any technology implementation. Any accessibility testing that starts without a solid plan and rationale will invariably fail in its implementation.

Rationale

Creating a rationale is similar to creating a business plan in many aspects. This will be the first thing that any accessibility tester in the future reads, and it will set the tone for the purpose and goals of any accessibility testing. A rationale can be on an organizational policy level, if you have the authority to do so, or it can be more of a personal statement of why you are doing it. It should also talk about all the library stakeholders who are affected by the testing, or who it will help and how you plan to include them. Finally, your rationale should talk about your methodology—a general statement about how you will go about conducting your testing.

Organizational or Personal Statement

If you are able to write on behalf of your organization or library, it is important to understand what is already written in your company policies about accessibility as well as any laws and statutes that particularly apply to you. A statement should give the reader the broad vision for why you care about accessibility and why it should matter. It is part persuasive argument and part explanation. This is the first thing someone will read and you want the reader to care about the results of your testing.

Library Stakeholders

Libraries are in a unique position as service institutions and exist for the benefit of, and by the will of, the people they serve. As a part of any project, it is important to do a quick survey of any people or groups of people who will be interested or impacted by your project. When it comes to accessibility testing, your list may include disabled patrons, community disability groups, local colleges and schools, the government, the library board of directors, and so forth. The amount of people that hold a stake in library website accessibility can be quite large because libraries exist for other people.

Methodology

The final piece of a rationale is explaining how you will conduct your testing. Considering that there is no single accessibility testing method, the easiest way to write a methodology is to pretend that you are explaining your testing process to individuals brand new to the

ORGANIZATIONAL STATEMENT EXAMPLE

"The important of library website accessibility is unparalleled. Your library is committed to making sure that our websites are accessible to *all* of our patrons, regardless of disability. To this end, we are instituting an annual accessibility audit of all of our websites to ensure that all our patrons have the same access to information."

STAKEHOLDER STATEMENT EXAMPLE

"Through our annual accessibility testing and audit, the library will ensure that all patrons have the same access to our online information. We will ensure that we comply with all laws and regulations regarding the Americans with Disabilities Act and Section 508. We aim to be WCAG 2.0 AA-level compliant, which means that our website is accessible for those using assistive technologies. We recognize that patrons and community disability groups have valuable insight to share and welcome all manner of feedback or volunteer testing in order that our website can help serve you better."

library. Keep it simple and short, but ensure that you give them enough information that they could go out and do something similar if they needed to.

Plan

Creating a testing plan is more in depth than just your methodology that you wrote for your rationale. The methodology is a good place to start when creating your plan. It can be easier to think about this like you were creating a project plan: it should clearly set out your goals and objectives, explain how you will assess your current state (including any tools needed for testing), note any failures and items that need action or follow up, explain how you will determine whether not you've met the goals that you set out, and then finally, it should explain what you will do going forward. A general accessibility testing plan outline will look something similar to this:

- Goals and objectives
- Test environment
- Tasks
- Action items
- Evaluation
- Reiteration

METHODOLOGY STATEMENT EXAMPLE

"This document is to provide a set process for testing Credo's e-learning objects, as well as guidance for how to analyze and report the testing results. To ensure consistent test situations, the test environment is provided as well as needed installations, and software or hardware requirements. For each of the WCAG 2.0 principles, there will be testing tasks that correspond with each of the sub-guidelines of each principle. There will also be a link to the corresponding sub-section of Section 508 for each testing task. Under the 'test analysis' section, normative standards and minimum compliance, along with recommended actions to be taken will be provided."

Goals and Objectives

When creating your goals and objectives, you must be very clear and specific. Goals should be SMART: specific, measurable, achievable, results focused, and time bound (University of Virginia n.d.):

- Specific: The goal must be clear what you want, or what you want patrons to be able to do. It must be narrow enough that it can be identified, as opposed to something too broad or overarching.
- Measurable: A good goal can be accurately measured so you can evaluate your progress. If your goal is that all patrons can access the library website, how will you be able to know whether you've met the goal? Is that goal really measurable?
- Achievable: Goals should be something realistic. It might be a stretch or it may be difficult and time consuming, but you know that it is something that is possible to do.
- Results focused: What is your goal going to do for the library? Will it increase your patron engagement? Drive usage or circulation statistics? What is the outcome that you expect to be able to put into a report?
- Time bound: Goals should have a realistic deadline. If you find that your goal cannot be completed in a realistic time frame, then you likely need to revise your goal as it is too broad. If you cannot put a deadline to your goal, try breaking the goal down into a few smaller goals and adding deadlines to those.

Test Environment

It is important to write down exactly what technical setup you are using to conduct your accessibility test. This is a standardization to ensure that you can replicate it again next

REAL-LIFE SCENARIO

Lucy was in charge of testing the accessibility of her new library news blog. She determined her goals for accessibility testing using the SMART method:

1. Objective: To increase the monthly average view of her blog within two months by ensuring that all patrons can access the blog.
2. Objective: To decrease the number of technical help emails that the library email receives by ensuring the website content is clearer and more navigable.
3. Objective: To increase the checkout of e-books and audiobooks by patrons compared to the previous month.

She knew that by testing for accessibility she could pay attention to both the content and the actual website technology to ensure that it is easily accessible by all patrons. She collected some initial statistics (from her blog views and the library circulation statistics), which she is using as a benchmark to measure her progress on her goals.

time or if others need to come in and do it, they will know what to expect. It is also important to keep your testing environment the same between tests (even if they are a year apart or more) because that ensures standardization. If you use one set of tools and your colleague completes her accessibility testing with another set of tools, you cannot know for sure whether the issues are a result of the differences in tools and computers, or actual accessibility failures. Ensuring that whoever completes accessibility tests uses the same testing tools eliminates that variable.

Testing environment notes can be short, but they generally should include what computer type or operating system to use, which browsers to test in, which screen readers to use, and specifically which testing tools to use.

Tasks

The tasks section of your accessibility testing plan will be the longest section. Which tasks you include depends on which standards you want to be compliant with and at which level. Generally WCAG 2.0 gives you tasks for each guideline and principle for the following levels: A, AA, and AAA. You should pick the tasks that are aligned at the level you desire to be. For a complete listing of WCAG 2.0 AA tasks (the compliance level that Section 508 requires), see appendix A.

When you write testing tasks, you need to ensure that they have a clear yes or no, success or failure result. For example, if you are working on Guideline 1.2 about time-based media (as in the scenario), a video either has captions or it doesn't. It either has an audio description or it doesn't. Those are easy yes/no options that you can add to a spreadsheet

REAL-LIFE SCENARIO

Based on the library's legal requirement to be WCAG 2.0 Level-AA compliant, Delonte needs to determine whether or not the library offers audio descriptions for all its pre-recorded audio with synchronized media. If not, he will mark it down as a criterion failure and identify steps to fix it. He also needs to make sure that they meet the lower requirement (Level A) of captions for all media. He uses the following WCAG guidelines to help him decide what his tasks should be assessing:

WCAG 2.0. Guideline 1.2 : Time-Based Media

- Level A, Success Criterion 1.2.2 Captions (Pre-recorded): Captions are provided for all pre-recorded audio content in synchronized media, except when the media is a media alternative for text and is clearly labeled as such.
- Level AA, Success Criterion 1.2.5 Audio Description (Pre-recorded): Audio description is provided for all pre-recorded video content in synchronized media.
- Level AAA, Success Criterion 1.2.6 Sign Language (Pre-recorded): Sign language interpretation is provided for all pre-recorded audio content in synchronized media.

or document to keep track of your testing tasks. See table 10.1 for an example accessibility testing spreadsheet. If a testing task results in a criterion failure, you need to highlight it or make note of it because you will come back to it when your testing is complete to set out action items.

Action Items

Once you've completed your testing, it is important to figure out what you will do with the information you get. You can have different follow-up options or to-do items for both successes and failures.

Failure Options

If you get a failure on a testing task or criterion, it doesn't mean that you stop there, throw your hands up, and say that your website isn't accessible. A failure in a task means that you need to do something to fix it. You must identify what needs to change so that the task will be a success next time.

Did a page of your website fail a color-ratio check? The action item on that task will be to change the colors on that page to ones with an acceptable ratio. Did it fail a closed-caption check? Then the action item for that will be to add closed captions to the video. Once you've created action items for each failure, it's important to actually follow

Table 10.1. Accessibility Testing Tasks

SUCCESS CRITERIA	LEVEL A	LEVEL AA	LEVEL AAA
Guideline 1.1: Text Alternatives **Criteria 1.1.1:** Non-text Content	All non-text content that is presented to the user has a text alternative that serves the equivalent purpose.		
Guideline 1.2: Time-Based Media **Criteria 1.2.2:** Captions (Prerecorded)	Captions are provided for all prerecorded audio content in synchronized media, except when the media is a media alternative for text and is clearly labeled as such.		
Guideline 1.2: Time-Based Media **Criteria 1.2.4:** Captions (Live)		Captions are provided for all live audio content in synchronized media.	
Guideline 1.2: Time-Based Media **Criteria 1.2.6:** Sign Language (Prerecorded)			Sign language interpretation is provided for all prerecorded audio content in synchronized media.

up and take the action. More than a simple "to-do list," action items can be split up into smaller items and can involve many people.

For instance, if your website failed the closed-caption check, your initial action item will be to add closed captions to the video. Once you start looking into it, however, you may realize that you'll need to involve the library's IT department to help, or that it needs to go through your line manager first. Each action item can turn into a mini-project, so it's important to fully think through each action item so it can be implemented.

Success Options

It's a common mistake to think that since a website has passed an accessibility check that there are no action items that result. The fact is, however, every success depends on its contextual situation: the time frame around it, current technologies, legal revisions, and levels of success.

A success during accessibility testing is only good for a short amount of time. Technology changes so quickly that online services and tools become obsolete really quickly. Just because your video player is working and showing the closed captions now doesn't mean that it will be working the same in three or six months. Technology reviews should happen at least every six months, just to ensure that everything is working as it should. If a service goes down or is no longer available, then you will need to set up alternate services.

Legal regulations are constantly being revised as well, and the general public typically is not notified of amendments or updates. As the accessibility tester, it is up to you to regularly check for legal updates. You should have a list of government and standards websites that you check for legal updates once or twice a year. That way you can keep ahead of any changes in regulations before you hear it as a complaint from a patron.

Finally, once you get a success on a testing task, it is important to decide whether the level of success is enough. If you've gotten success criteria on all the Level A WCAG 2.0 tasks, you need to realize that isn't enough—you have to have successes on the Level AA tasks as well. If you've passed all the Level AA tasks, perhaps it's time to put in some extra effort to try to start meeting the Level AAA tasks. A success criteria does not mean that your work is done. A website can *always* be more accessible.

Evaluation

Once you've finished the testing, completed your tasks, and the website is accessible, it's important to reflect back on your testing process to see how you can improve it for next time. No project is complete without some time spent at the end thinking about what went well, what didn't go so well, and what you can do better next time.

The program evaluation doesn't need to be formal or even very in depth. In businesses, these are called retrospectives, where you come away from a project with what you learned and ways to do it better next time. Retrospectives are useful practices because they are so versatile—once you find a format that works well for you, you can re-use it for any project or program that you want to evaluate.

WANT TO KNOW MORE?

Appendix A includes sample evaluation and retrospective forms that you can use to start evaluating your accessibility tasks.

Reiteration

The final step in the accessibility testing process is to do it again. Once a website meets the accessibility guidelines, it doesn't promise that it will always meet them. New content can be added to a website that is non-accessible, accessibility standards may change, or new assistive technology may become available.

A good time frame for setting up a recurring accessibility test is yearly. Doing it on an annual basis allows enough time for new laws to be enacted and new content to be added to the website. When you repeat an accessibility test, however, you must start fresh. You cannot use the data from the previous test. Just because your closed captions worked last year does not mean that they still work.

Committing to accessibility is an ongoing commitment, not something that is completed and done. It is an evolving project, with many individual components that change in their own rate. Accessibility is partially a mind-set and partially action: you must think about accessibility and you must do something about it.

Automated Testing

Accessibility testing is a big project, and there are many online applications and software downloads that can automate some of the accessibility testing process. These automated tools can help identify coding errors, missing image descriptions, and other HTML-specific accessibility items that can be difficult to test manually.

Automated Testing Tools

These tools come in a variety of formats, including stand-alone software downloads, bookmarklets, browser plug-ins, and even online applications. Depending on how comfortable you are with HTML and web programming, there is a tool for you. Some tools use API calls and can be very technical and in depth, while others simply ask you to type in the URL and the program does the rest. The following is a list of the different types of automated accessibility testers, along with the most popular programs.

Bookmarklets and Browser Plug-Ins

- Pixo and the University of Illinois at Urbana-Champaign Bookmarklet
- Google Chrome Accessibility Developer Tools
- WAVE Chrome and Firefox Extensions
- ARIA Validator for Chrome

Online Testing Applications

- HTML CodeSniffer
- WAVE Accessibility Tool
- Tenon

Stand-Alone Software

- PayPal's Automated Accessibility Testing Tool
- Bureau of Internet Accessibility Testing Service
- Cynthia Says

When using automated testing software, it is important to remember that it is a starting point—in no way is automation a substitute for manual testing. You cannot run your website through one of these checkers and then claim it's accessible. These automated accessibility testing websites and programs will help you to identify basic accessibility issues right off the bat, or ones that you will not be able to identify during manual testing. They will give you a broad overview of the coding behind the website and can help identify missing image alternative descriptions, missing ARIA tags, and how the website is structured.

Manual Testing

Once you've used an automated accessibility testing program and fixed any issues it noted, your next step is to manually test with some of the most common different types of assistive technologies: keyboard access, screen readers, no style sheets, and voice commands.

Keyboard Access Testing

Testing whether a website is fully accessible via keyboard (with no mouse) covers the most ground for accessibility testing. If you remember from the types of assistive technology in the first half of this book, a majority of assistive technologies are based on keyboard access. Switches, a foot mouse, the sip-and-puff, and many others use the same conduits as keyboard controls. If your website is accessible via the keyboard, it should be accessible for all the other assistive navigational technologies as well.

Keyboard testing is also one of the easiest types of accessibility testing, since it doesn't require any software or additional tools. To test how a website is navigated via keyboard, simply place your mouse cursor in the browser URL address bar, then take your hand off the mouse and do not use it again. Keyboard navigation typically uses Tab to move forward, Shift-Tab to move backward, up/down arrows to scroll, and the return or space bar to select something.

If a website includes interactions that react differently to keyboard strokes, such as drag and drop items, or dropdown menus, then the website should provide instructions about which keyboard keys the user will need to use. There are some specific items to look for when testing keyboard navigation, including focus, structure, and links.

Focus

When you navigate a website using the keyboard, it is vital to understand which item on the screen the keyboard is interacting with. This is usually shown with a small box around the item or area. If a hyperlink has the focus, it should show in the hover state, as it would if you were hovering the mouse cursor over it.

When testing, you need to make sure that you don't get caught in what is called a keyboard trap. Keyboard traps are areas of a web page that can trap the keyboard in a separate navigation than the outer web page. This can often happen with Flash applications or other embedded multimedia, by allowing users to press Tab to enter the area, but when they press Tab or ESC to try to exit the area, they cannot reach the main window navigation again. Another type of keyboard trap is through a particular use of JavaScript that uses key presses as an event trigger. In that case, with a list of two links, any key pressed will trigger the first link and the user cannot get past it to focus on the second link (Stringer 2011). It traps them in a cyclical process. Keyboard traps are important enough (and foundational enough to accessibility itself) that the WCAG 2.0 standards count it as a success criterion (W3C n.d.).

Structure

While testing navigation via keyboard, it is important to notice the structure of the web page and in which order your keyboard focus moves. Using a logical structure, the keyboard focus should start in the top left of the web page, and move right and then down. Unless you are testing a website that relies on a language that reads right to left, the keyboard focus should always move top to bottom and left to right.

The structure should also make sense for the website as a whole. If there is a list of links on the left side of every page with content in the middle, then the keyboard focus should first show a "Skip to Main Content" link (which would make it go straight to the main content, not the list of links) and then focus on each of the navigation links on the left, and then the main content on the right. If the website structure is off or non-logical, you will not be able to predict where the keyboard will navigate you to next.

Links

For sighted users, links are a part of the background of a website and something they can scan over or ignore if they desire. Users who use keyboards to navigate a web page do not have the option to ignore a section of the website. It is imperative that each website offer this option to ignore long lists of links by the inclusion of a "Skip to Main Content" link. This will allow the keyboard focus to skip the long lists of navigation links and go straight to the page's main content.

When testing links using a keyboard, it is important to ensure that the links do not end up with a keyboard trap, and that once you click on a link, you can navigate past it with the keyboard.

Screen Readers

Testing with screen readers is an important part of accessibility testing, but it takes time to understand how screen readers work. If you test a website without spending the time to understand the screen reader first, it is likely that most of the errors you run into will be user errors instead of actual accessibility failures.

COMMON SCREEN READER SOFTWARE

- JAWS (Jobs Access with Speech)
- NVDA (NonVisual Desktop Access)
- Apple VoiceOver (Mac software)
- Orca (Linux software)
- WebbIE (online browser software)

Low Internet Testing

A quick way to see the visual structure of your website along with missing image tags is by turning style sheets (CSS) off in your browser. This will turn a regular website into plain text on a white background. This makes any "skip to content" link visible and you can see the order of items that a screen reader will read. Depending on which browser you use, the capability may be built in or you may need an extension.

Once the style sheet is turned off, you should scan the order of links and sections on the page, keeping in mind that this is what the screen reader will be reading and what the keyboard will use to navigate. You should also scan for missing image tags, as they are also visible when style sheets are turned off.

Voice Navigation Testing

You can test how the website responds to voice-activated navigation by downloading and using a voice recognition software. There are many software options available as well as options that come built in to the Windows and Mac operating systems. The most commonly used voice recognition options are:

- Windows Speech Recognition: Built in for Windows
- Dictation: Built in for Mac
- Dragon NaturallySpeaking: Third party for Windows or Mac
- Voice Finger: Third party for Windows

When setting up a new voice recognition software, it is vital that you spend some time training the computer to recognize your speech patterns. Every person has a different accent and different speech patterns. You need to train the computer to recognize what you say and correct it when it misunderstands.

Keep in mind that illnesses, dental issues, or other facial changes may change your voice and speech patterns so much that the computer may no longer recognize what you say. If that happens, you will need to re-train it to your new speech patterns (if it will be a long amount of time).

Testing by Disabled People

When setting out your accessibility testing plan, it is important to include disabled patrons as much as possible. Meet with them and listen to their concerns about the library's website accessibility, or use a survey to gather data. Many organizations for disabled people have accessibility/usability testing groups as well as resources that can help you set up your test in the correct manner. If you do not have any community groups or organizations in your community, you may need to recruit your accessibility testers yourself.

Organizational Testing Groups

If you contract with an accessibility testing group that employs disabled people to test websites, you will need to pay special attention to the rules and regulations of that particular organization. Each organization will have its own procedure and process to follow, which ensures the safety of its employees.

This can be a great way to gather real-time feedback from disabled computer users and to see how a host of assistive technologies work.

Self-Recruited Testing Groups

Recruiting your own disabled patrons for accessibility testers can be rewarding, but also fraught with difficulties. If you are not careful, you could easily discriminate or offend someone without meaning to. If you recruit your own volunteers, you will need to have a very clear idea of what outcomes you want as well as the tasks and activities that you will ask your users to complete.

In a sense, you will be using members of the public to conduct user testing in a focus group. In a focus group, however, there is an unspecified promise for change. Be aware that by engaging patrons in a focus group you are entering into an unspoken contract: your patrons expect something for their time and effort (namely, changes to the website) and you expect to get user stories and evidence to use in your accessibility case. Nothing is ever free, and the time and labor of a group that has very little to spare is especially valuable. Give their effort the respect it deserves by constructing a proper focus group or user testing.

Focus Groups

A focus group is a small group interview about a particular topic. It is a method of conducting qualitative research and can add to a body of evidence about a certain issue. Focus groups typically involve a moderated interview or open discussion with fewer than ten participants in order to learn their views about a topic. When including a sensitive or underserved population, you should take great care to adhere to best practices for focus groups. Your patrons are doing you a great service.

BEST PRACTICES FOR RUNNING A FOCUS GROUP

- Be respectful: Respect participants' stories and lived experiences.
- Be transparent: Tell participants the goals and results, if any.
- Be prepared: Prepare your questions in advance and imagine what could happen in the group.
- Use the data: Your participants have given their time and effort; you have an obligation to give them results and feedback.

REAL-LIFE SCENARIO

Jose is a user services librarian at a large public library in Chicago. He is in charge of redesigning the Online Resources web page and has designed a user experience test. He put out a call for participants in the local newspaper and designed the test around three main tasks that patrons most often need to complete when first going to the web page. He asked his participants to complete the following tasks:

- Locate the online resources from the library homepage.
- Check out an e-book.
- Locate a news article in the *Chicago Tribune* from 1875.
- Find homework help for an elementary school child.

User Testing

User testing differs from focus groups in many ways, but generally is a more precise instrument to capture data about how a particular user interacts with a website. During a user experience test, the test moderator sets out specific tasks that the user must complete (e.g., check out an e-book or find the library opening hours) and watches how the user completes the tasks and identifies the problems that the user faced and how she overcame the obstacles.

User testing can be live, where the user is watched by a member of the user testing group, or can be asynchronous, where software is used that records what a user does on his home computer screen, which is then watched at a later time by the user testing group. All of this is done ethically and with *consent* and full knowledge of what the user should expect. It is vital that you lay out clear tasks and expectations for the user to be in compliance with laws regarding human subjects.

Accessibility Statements and Documents

Ensuring that patrons can access websites is important, but it is just as important to ensure that they know there are options for disabled patrons. Most websites require an Accessibility page that explains the options that disabled patrons have in accessing and interacting with the web page. Accessibility pages should mention the WCAG level of compliance, along with a contact number for any accessibility trouble. It should also include unique accessibility items, such as specific keyboard commands, or how to interact with widgets (like drag and drop items) via the keyboard.

Key Points

While this chapter covered a lot of best practices for accessibility testing, the most important thing to remember is that you are willing to admit that your website needs accessibility fixes. They say that admitting that you have a problem is half the battle—once you've realized that you need to make changes, accessibility testing is simply a method to find out exactly what changes you need to make. Key points to remember:

- Good accessibility testing processes should start with a plan, goals, and objectives.
- Be sure to include patrons with disabilities as much as possible in focus groups or user testing.
- If the website fails an accessibility criterion, it is not the end but rather the beginning of changes.

Further Resources

Automated Testing Resources

Bookmarklets and Browser Plug-Ins:

- Pixo and the University of Illinois at Urbana-Champaign Bookmarklet: http://accessibility-bookmarklets.org/
- Google Chrome Accessibility Developer Tools: https://chrome.google.com/webstore/detail/accessibility-developer-t/fpkknkljclfencbdbgkenhalefipecmb?hl=en
- WAVE Chrome and Firefox Extensions: http://wave.webaim.org/extension/
- ARIA Validator for Chrome: https://chrome.google.com/webstore/detail/aria-validator/oigghlanfjgnkcndchmnlnmaojahnjoc

Online Testing Applications

- HTML CodeSniffer: http://squizlabs.github.io/HTML_CodeSniffer/
- WAVE Accessibility Tool: http://wave.webaim.org/
- Tenon: https://tenon.io

Stand-Alone Software

- PayPal's Automated Accessibility Testing Tool: https://github.com/paypal/AATT/blob/master/README.md
- Bureau of Internet Accessibility Testing Service: http://www.boia.org/wc3-free-2-0-aa-report
- Cynthia Says: http://www.cynthiasays.com/

Manual Testing Resources

Screen Readers

- JAWS: http://www.freedomscientific.com/Products/Blindness/JAWS
- VoiceOver: https://help.apple.com/voiceover/info/guide/10.12/
- NVDA: https://www.nvaccess.org/
- Orca: https://help.gnome.org/users/orca/stable/introduction.html.en
- WebbIE: http://www.webbie.org.uk/

Voice Recognition Software

- Windows Speech Recognition: https://support.microsoft.com/en-us/help/17208/windows-10-use-speech-recognition
- Dictation (Apple/Mac): https://support.apple.com/en-gb/HT202584
- Dragon NaturallySpeaking: http://www.nuance.co.uk/dragon/index.htm
- Voice Finger: http://voicefinger.cozendey.com/

Focus Group and User Testing Resources

- International Association for Public Participation: http://www.iap2.org/
- Kansas University's Community Toolbox: http://ctb.ku.edu/en/assessing-community-needs-and-resources
- Usability How-Tos: https://www.usability.gov/how-to-and-tools/index.html

References

Stringer, Dan. 2011."Keyboard Traps." *Humanising Technology Blog*. April 13, 2011. https://www.nomensa.com/blog/2011/keyboard-traps.

University of Virginia. n.d. "Writing S.M.A.R.T. Goals." Accessed June 15, 2017. http://www.hr.virginia.edu/uploads/documents/media/Writing_SMART_Goals.pdf.

W3C. n.d. "Understanding Success Criterion 2.1.2." Accessed June 20, 2017. https://www.w3.org/TR/UNDERSTANDING-WCAG20/keyboard-operation-trapping.html.

CHAPTER 11

Third-Party and Library Vendor Websites

IN THIS CHAPTER

- ▷ Creating and implementing a communication plan
- ▷ Negotiating with a third party to make accessibility changes on its website
- ▷ Best practices for advocacy and negotiation

IT IS A DIFFICULT BUT NECESSARY TASK to ensure that third-party websites meet accessibility standards. By evaluating library databases and external websites, librarians ensure that their disabled patrons have the same access to information as non-disabled patrons. The process of evaluating a third-party or library vendor website, however, can be fraught with tension and insecurity.

This chapter gives you best practices for partnering with third parties to ensure that their website is accessible for your patrons. It covers both library vendors and other entities, and gives real-world examples of what works and what doesn't.

Advocacy Road Map

After you've completed an accessibility test on a third-party website, it is tempting to start advocating for change immediately, especially if the failures are particularly egregious. Jumping right into advocacy without stopping to consider the issues and organizations involved will always lead to poorer results. Before you can start actively advocating for accessible changes, it is important to complete a series of pre-advocacy tasks:

- Research the organization.
- Identify internal and external stakeholders.

- Consider alternate points of view.
- Create a plan.
- Reiterate.

Research

Before you can start asking a library vendor to change something on its website, you need to fully be aware about what drives the company. Organizational research can be time consuming, but the payoffs are well worth the time invested. Before you do anything, it's important to spend a few minutes compiling a small company profile that includes the organizational goals, key people within the company, and current press releases. There are many ways to conduct organizational research, but the ones that yield the most fruit are support pages, the corporate website, library databases, internet search engines, and social media.

Conducting background research on a company is a skill that is useful in many contexts, not just advocating for accessibility changes. When you conduct your company research, understanding how the company relates to its customers can help you position yourself as a partner and advocate for accessibility.

Support Pages

The very first place you should look for information about how vendors deal with accessibility is their support pages. Looking here first will immediately let you know if they've addressed the request already, in which case you may just need to update your subscription or patch your platform. If they haven't dealt with your specific accessibility request before, looking at their support pages is a great way to get a sense of their level of customer support. Are the support pages incredibly bare? You may have a difficult time ahead of you. Are they chock full of information or customer messages? In that case, they might have a great customer support mentality. How a company deals with customer support can make or break an accessibility initiative, so it is important to understand the lay of the land before you make any plans.

The Corporate Website

One of the first places you should look for company information is on the corporate website. You can typically glean a vast amount of information by looking for the "About Us" link. This page will give you publicly available information about the company's history, its management, vision statement, and (if you're lucky) policies or related standards.

If the website doesn't have an "About Us" link, you can look for other links on their web page that might offer similar information, like Investor Relations, Careers, Privacy Policy, or even the Contact Us page. You can gather enough information across these links to create a basic company profile by filling out the journalistic questions: who, what, when, why, where, and how.

Library Databases

It is helpful to check library databases for business competitive intelligence, as this information can be more in depth than information found on the open web. Common library databases are:

- Hoover's Online
- Mergent Online
- Factiva
- Reference USA
- BusinessInsider

If you are unable to access a library database for corporate intelligence, there are plenty of database websites that you can access via the open web. The information within these databases will need to be evaluated as would any information you glean from the internet:

- Bloomberg
- EDGAR (The U.S. SEC Filing Database)
- Glassdoor
- Crunchbase
- Better Business Bureau

Internet Search Engines

As useful as library databases and company information sites are, they do not provide you with the broader overview of all of a company's activities. For the broad overview, it is important to search for the company in an internet search engine. Doing this will provide you with a broad array of information, from the company's social media feed to court cases it may not publicize on its corporate website.

In addition to an internet search, you should take a quick look at the results within national or industry news websites as well. If the company is looking at a merger, filing for bankruptcy, or involved in a lengthy legal dispute, the news sites should let you know. This broad information can give you the basics of the health and activity of a company.

Social Media

Somewhat newer to the business intelligence research field are social media feeds. Regardless of how pristine the planned social media policy is, the community-centered and very real-life nature of social media means that you can gather pertinent information about how the company interacts with its consumers. There are many forms of social media that can connect you with information about a company. For instance:

- LinkedIn
- Facebook
- Twitter

When conducting research on social media, just be sure to evaluate any information that you get for bias and assumptions. There are plenty of online research help manuals that can guide you to discipline-specific websites, but again, be sure to evaluate the bias of each guide.

Identify Stakeholders

Once you've researched the company and compiled a basic profile, it's important to make a list of all the stakeholders involved in your accessibility issue. A stakeholder, generally, is someone who has a "vested interest or concern in a particular issue" (Scheffran 2006, 154). The wide-net approach to interested bodies includes both an upside and a downside: the upside is that you will ensure that you list everyone who would be affected by the accessibility issue, and the downside is that the more people involved in an issue, the longer it takes to resolve it. Common stakeholders for an accessibility issue are:

- Library patrons
- Library staff
- Local and state government
- Company employees
- Company executives
- Company shareholders/board members
- Disability advocacy groups

Stakeholders can be broken up into different groups and by different categories, depending on how you would like to categorize them. They can be internal or external to an organization, have high or low urgency, hold power or not, and many more. Be sure to categorize your stakeholders into only the categories you feel will help your analysis—too many categories lessens the impact of a stakeholder analysis.

Consider Different Points of View

When your stakeholder list is complete, take a few moments and write a small paragraph explaining the accessibility issue from their point of view. The accessibility issue will look very different to the CEO of a company than it does to a blind consumer.

Being able to consider different points of view is a central tenet of problem solving, as it helps you to think of different solutions that you may not have originally considered. If you are unsure of a stakeholder's point of view, you should ask the stakeholder—especially for the under-represented stakeholders, like disabled people. Their voices and stories are often co-opted by mainstream media, so it is important to give them a place to tell their own stories and have their voice be heard.

Create a Plan

By this point, you've completed all your research, organized your thoughts about different perspectives, and identified all the people who have a stake in the issue. It is now time to create your action plan for communication. If you communicate with the vendor without any sort of plan, your accessibility initiative will end up buried in an email in-box and nothing will get done.

Timeline

Creating a communication timeline follows the same general steps as creating a project plan for any task that you have to complete. You need to think about your objectives, a timeline, what actions you will take, who you will contact (and in what order), and what you will do if it all fails.

REAL-LIFE SCENARIO

A sample communication timeline could look like the following:

- June 1: Email the customer support email.
- June 10: If no response, call customer support.
- June 15: If escalation is needed, email company officers.
- June 30: Get external stakeholders to email the company to provide weight to request.
- July 15: Evaluate progress and revise plan if needed.

Identify Your Success Markers

When creating your communication plan, it is important to identify what, exactly, success means for you. Will you count it a success only if the library vendor changes its website to fix the accessibility issue? Is it a success if you do your job to advocate for your patrons and at least get the company thinking about accessibility? Depending on what your objectives are will help determine what steps you take in your communication plan.

Engage in Dialogue

No problem worth solving is solved easily. This goes doubly when there are multiple organizations and stakeholders involved. An accessibility issue with a website is typically not a quick or easy fix—the company needs to evaluate the time and expense that it will take to fix the issue and compare it with its own internal priorities. Oftentimes, however unfortunate, accessibility fixes just don't compete with moneymaking priorities. That is why it is important to understand that any negotiation with a library vendor about an accessibility fix will be a dialogue.

As the initiator, it is your responsibility to offer a powerful argument for why making the accessibility fix will be a good thing for the company. But effective communication also includes listening (North 2016) because there are always more than two sides to any single issue. To get to a solution with the vendor, you need to advocate for change, but you also must listen and understand the company's point of view. There may be other issues standing in the way of the company fixing the accessibility issue, or it may already have it slated to be fixed in a future update. Go into the dialogue with an open mind, because vendors typically desire their customers to be satisfied with the product.

Active Listening

As important as it is for you to present your case, it is just as vital to be an active listener when the library vendor speaks. Active listening is finding meaning and making sense of what you hear (Gannon-Leary and McCarthy 2010, ch. 6). Meaning can be found by keeping an open mind, asking questions to clarify points, and restating what you've understood. Being an active listener when it comes to dialogue with library vendors means that you will better understand the company's position and there will be a better, more open line of communication between you.

Constructive Speaking

The counterpoint to active listening is constructive speaking. During the course of a dialogue, your role will constantly change from listener to speaker, depending on the context, and it is important that you practice skills for both.

Constructive speaking is a method of talking where both parties benefit. It reduces confusions, and helps the listener to better understand your point of view. Tips for constructive speaking are:

- Be clear and concise.
- Understand your biases and assumptions.
- Be positive.
- Check for understanding.
- Reiterate.

Do It Again

An accessibility initiative is never complete. If you've been successful in partnering with the company to change its website to solve one accessibility issue, you may be able to partner with the company to identify other accessibility issues within its website. The company benefits from this as you are doing unpaid work that its employees now no longer need to do, you benefit because you are serving your patrons better, and your patrons benefit because the vendor website is more accessible.

Central Tenets of Advocacy

When it comes to asking library vendors or third parties to make their websites more accessible, it is vitally important to remember that you are in a position of advocacy for your disabled patrons. Advocacy is "the process of pleading a cause or supporting a proposal" (*Merriam-Webster* n.d.). You are not a lawyer trying to prosecute a negligent company—you are trying to enact change on behalf of your patrons. When you advocate for something, it is important to consider the central tenets of advocacy in planning your communication strategy, along with what works and what doesn't work. The central tenets are:

- Mutual exchange
- Market forces
- Shared values
- Framing
- The inverse care law
- Showing evidence to power

The Principle of Mutual Exchange

The principle of mutual exchange is often more colloquially known as "quid pro quo" or "this for that." In effect, you are giving something of value to get something that you want.

You will have a much higher advocacy success rate if you can place a tangible value on the change that you desire, whether that is money, time, or reputation.

While it may sound like bribery initially, many things in the professional world work on this principle of mutual exchange. Even the fundamental task of marketing boils down to promising benefits after a purchase. When you consider what you can offer in a mutual exchange, it's important to remember that many concepts that are free or low value to you (such as your time, effort, and words) have high values to vendors.

Money

Businesses often offer more customization or product support at higher purchase levels. While the legal level of accessibility should come along with the basic product, if you want a higher level of accessibility, it may be worth looking into the product support or customization packages that the company has to offer. It will come down to a whether the change you want is worth the price.

Time

Free labor has its own professional currency in the business world. All businesses struggle with balancing labor costs with revenue to some extent. Getting work completed for free is a powerful motivator for businesses because they can then leverage that completed work for further sales. If you offer to continue accessibility testing for them, that is one thing they don't have to use their own employees for and something they can monetize and market later on. It's a win-win scenario.

Reputation

Reputation is a very important currency within any industry. The library industry is full of well-known names of both libraries and library vendors. Even if your library isn't a well-known name, it still carries worth. Many companies like to use successful customer stories as case studies or white papers for their marketing. If you are comfortable publicizing your partnership with the vendor, most companies will love to use the story for their marketing campaigns.

REAL-LIFE SCENARIO

Jean's library created a set of sign language "how-to" videos for its most popular online resources. She wanted to add them to the library's video stream side by side with the regular spoken and captioned videos. That way, her deaf patrons would have a choice on how they wanted to view the video. The library website's streaming service only allows one video per page, but Jean noticed that for a few extra dollars per month, she could have the ability to include more than one video per page. In her mind, the exchange was worth it—more customization and accessibility for a small price.

REAL-LIFE SCENARIO

Kyong is a librarian at a small-town public library in Iowa. She is working with a library vendor to make sure it adds a "skip to content" link at the top of its website. During the course of her communication with customer support, she mentioned that she is always happy to provide a case study or quote for marketing.

Market Forces

The important thing to know about market forces when it comes to accessibility advocacy is that everything has its price. The forces of supply and demand typically work out the ideal price for a product, so if you are asking for accessibility changes that will not make any change in the demand for a product, it may be difficult for the vendor to see a business case to make the change.

If, on the other hand, you can create an argument that affects either the supply or the demand, the vendor will be more open to consider the changes. In the information age, products are not simply manufactured, so supply typically relates more to the labor involved in the product. If a company has fewer employees available, it will be more limited in its supply.

Soft Skills

Some of the central tenets of advocacy are often considered "soft skills." These are skills like communication, leadership, critical thinking, and other traits that are difficult to define and evaluate. These communication skills can be used to create and bolster an accessibility argument, without turning it into an "us versus them" situation. Two of these communication and critical thinking skills are vitally important to advocacy: shared values and framing a problem.

Shared Values

When creating an argument for a debate, it is important to define the different sides of the debate. When you are advocating, however, it is important that you start defining what both

REAL-LIFE SCENARIO

Jorge is trying to convince a library vendor to add closed captions to its videos. The videos currently do not have any captions at all and are the only item that makes the product not meet WCAG Level AA standards. Jorge realizes that the library vendor may not be aware that federally funded institutions (like libraries) have to meet AA standards. While writing up his communication plan, he makes sure to include the fact that if libraries become aware of the product not meeting the AA standards, they may cancel because they could lose their federal funding otherwise, thus decreasing the demand for the product.

REAL-LIFE SCENARIO

Ash is a customer support representative for a small library vendor that sells videos about information literacy. He received a support ticket from a librarian customer who complained about a lack of an accessibility feature. Normally he would just put this into the vendor's feature request logbook, but the customer then went on to describe how important information literacy is to disadvantaged groups of people. Disabled people have an incredible need for information literacy skills, and making this accessibility change will help them to access the videos and learn more about information literacy. This discussion about the shared value of information literacy spurred Ash to take it directly to the product manager himself, and it was quickly implemented and then turned into a marketing story.

sides have in common, instead of identifying the differences first. By starting with a positive outlook and defining shared values, it will set a different tone to all your communication. Instead of seeming argumentative or antagonistic, if you focus on values that are shared between the library vendor and your library, you will come across as positive and professional.

By focusing on shared values, you can position yourself as a partner to the library vendor in support of a certain goal. This is where company research can come in handy. Once you know what the library vendor stands for—what it lists on its mission and vision statements, what you can glean from its "About Us" page, and any information you can gather from employee reviews—will help you to find something that you have in common and can help support your accessibility goals.

Framing a Problem

The process of framing a problem is a major part of critical thinking. We often do this without fully being aware of it. Any time you take a larger problem and focus in on a smaller detail, you are framing that detail as the problem. It's easy to think of it taking a small picture frame and placing it over different places of a larger picture—it brings those details into focus.

When you are framing an intellectual or conceptual problem (such as website accessibility), it's not so much a matter of framing different places but rather framing different aspects of the problem. When you are creating your argument or communication plan, take your mental picture frame and place it over different aspects of the problem: If you focused on just video closed captions, how would that change the overall argument? What would happen to your argument if you enlarged the picture frame to encompass all multimedia, not just video captions?

Each of these different ways of looking at the problem is simply shifting the mental picture frame to place something else at the center of the problem. It can help you to identify a more holistic and better solution.

The Inverse Care Law

The inverse care law is a health care principle of thought that originated in Wales in the 1970s. A doctor proposed that "the availability of good medical care tends to vary *inversely* with the need for the populations served" (Dalrymple 2012). This medical principle can be extended to accessibility in websites by saying that "the availability of information access online tends to vary *inversely* with the need for information." To put it simply, those population groups who most desperately need information are the most unlikely to be able to access it.

It is important to keep this in mind when advocating for website accessibility because it's not simply a matter of complying with legal statues, but often a case of some of the most in-need population groups desperately seeking information (often for health or subsistence reasons) but unable to gain access. The inverse care law helps to remind you that while it may be a matter of life or death to your disabled patrons, website accessibility may not even be a blip on the radar for many businesses. It is up to you to argue for website accessibility so those who need information can access it.

Showing Evidence to Power

One of the common phrases that has gained traction in recent times is "speaking truth to power." This phrase constantly pops up at protests and advocacy gatherings and, actually, is not new at all. It appears to originate from a Quaker pamphlet advocating pacifism in 1955 (Quaker.org n.d.) but seems to have taken on new life as an advocacy slogan. The problem with it, however, is that truth is subjective; the truth for a blind patron who can't access a website is vastly different from the truth for a business that is focused on profit.

The sentiment behind the slogan is valid, but perhaps the slogan should be altered a bit. Instead of "speaking truth" to power, perhaps we should focus on "showing evidence" to power. The shift in focus from subjective truth to objective evidence means that it is easier to back up your argument if you're already thinking about the evidence. Compiling evidence to show to those in power to make changes is both good business sense and scientifically sound. While you cannot control what they do with the evidence that you submit, you've contributed to the corpus of work surrounding an issue, which helps those who come after you advocating for the same subject.

One political analyst noted that "power is in pieces, which resist picking up, and truth is partial, resistant to being made whole" (Wildavsky 1987, 401). This was true in 1987 and remains true to this day. Truth is only valid in an argument if both sides agree that it's the truth. Using evidence, instead of truth, to underpin your argument is something that both sides agree on as valid. Build your case with evidence—from your market research to your research into laws and statutes—and you will be speaking a language that both you and the library vendor understand.

There are many common ways to frame problems (Idea Sandbox, n.d.), but the most common are:

- Time: What will this look like in three, six, or twelve months?
- Resources: What would the problem look like if we had unlimited resources? What does it look like on our current resources?
- Stakeholders: What does the problem look like to the library vendor? To the blind patron? To the library itself?

Key Points

While website accessibility may be very important to you, it may not be as important to other companies. Librarians must often act as advocates for the needs of their patrons, and advocating for accessibility changes on a library vendor's website is often necessary. Key points to remember:

- Do your research on both the company and the issue before starting any communication.
- Use evidence and market forces (free labor and supply and demand) to strengthen your argument.
- Advocates speak for change, but they also listen to the other side. Practice your communication and active listening skills.

Further Resources

Free Company Research Resources

- Bloomberg: http://www.bloomberg.com/research/company/overview/overview.asp
- EDGAR (The U.S. SEC Filing Database): https://www.sec.gov/edgar/searchedgar/webusers.htm
- Glassdoor: https://www.glassdoor.co.uk/Reviews/index.htm
- Crunchbase: https://www.crunchbase.com/#/home/index
- Better Business Bureau: https://www.bbb.org/

Paid/Library Company Research Resources

- Hoover's Online
- Mergent Online
- Factiva
- Reference USA
- BusinessInsider

The Central Tenets of Advocacy

- Mutual exchange
- Market forces
- Shared values
- Framing
- The inverse care law
- Showing evidence to power

References

Dalrymple, Theodore. 2012. "The Inverse Care Law." *BMJ* 344 (March 7, 2012). doi:10.1136/bmj.e1633.

Gannon-Leary, Pat, and Michael D. McCarthy. 2010. "Questioning and Active Listening." In *Customer Care*, 83–99. Oxford, UK: Chandos. doi:10.1016/B978-1-84334-570-1.50006-1.

Idea Sandbox. n.d. "Better Problem Solving with Framing." Accessed July 25, 2017. https://idea-sandbox.com/blog/frame-your-problems-to-create-better-solutions/.

Merriam-Webster. n.d. S.v. "Advocacy." Accessed July 25, 2017. https://www.merriam-webster.com/dictionary/advocacy.

North, Marjorie. 2016. "Mastering the Basics of Communication." Harvard Division of Continuing Education. https://www.extension.harvard.edu/professional-development/blog/mastering-basics-communication.

Scheffran, Jürgen. 2006. "Tools for Stakeholder Assessment and Interaction." In *Stakeholder Dialogues in Natural Resources Management: Theory and Practice*, edited by Susanne Stollkleemann and Martin Welp, 153–85. Berlin, Heidelberg: Springer Berlin Heidelberg. doi:10.1007/978-3-540-36917-2_6.

Quaker.org. n.d. "Speak Truth to Power." Originally published March 2, 1955. http://www.quaker.org/sttp.html.

Wildavsky, Aaron. 1987. *Speaking Truth to Power: The Art and Craft of Policy Analysis*. 2nd ed. New Brunswick, NJ: Transaction.

CHAPTER 12

Beyond Accessibility

Moving toward Universal Design

IN THIS CHAPTER

- ▷ How to think beyond technical accessibility
- ▷ Nielsen's ten heuristics of usability
- ▷ The seven principles of universal design
- ▷ How to take a person-centered approach

Beyond Accessibility

IF YOU'VE GONE THROUGH THIS BOOK, followed all the testing checklists and recommended steps, and made a nicely accessible website, good job! Go ahead, sit back, and give yourself a nice little pat on the back. Then get motivated because there are still things to do to make your website more accessible to even more people—you didn't think that was it, did you?

Just as oppression and advocacy never end, your job as an advocate of equitable access to online information will also never end. While there are things beyond the scope of this book that you can do, this final chapter will give you a brief foot in the door of three items to focus on once you've gotten past the technical accessibility of your website:

- The ten heuristics of usability
- The seven principles of universal design
- The person-centered approach

Nielsen's Ten Usability Heuristics

Jakob Nielsen pioneered usability as it related to technology when it became an emerging field in the mid-nineties. He is most known for his usability heuristics (or "rules of thumb") that he set down in 1994. These heuristics are still often taught in library school programs today.

You may notice that some of these sound familiar. That is because they have been distilled and encoded into accessibility standards and laws that we've already discussed extensively. Nielsen (1995) put forth ten usability heuristics that, if followed, would generally lend a much more pleasant user experience. A heuristic, known more as a rule of thumb, is something that will get you results quicker than being exact. You know the maxim "Perfect is the enemy of good"? If you aim to be perfect in everything you do, it will take too long and you'll never make any progress. Heuristics are small, easily digestible chunks of common wisdom about a topic whereby you can gauge where your website falls on the scale of usability and find areas that you might need to spend more time working on.

Each heuristic listed below gives a small definition and a list of WCAG 2.0 accessibility standards (W3C n.d.) that fit with that heuristic, showing you that accessibility and usability really are just two sides of the same coin.

Visibility of System Status

The system should always be sending appropriate feedback and status updates to the user so that the user always knows what is going on with the task and how long is left in the process.

This visibility of system status heuristic is consistent with one WCAG 2.0 standard:

- Guideline 2.4: Provide ways to help users navigate, find content, and determine where they are.

Match between System and the Real World

Language and items should be familiar to the user and follow a familiar order. This is why one of the most common and universal icons on a computer screen is a trash can icon—something that translates almost universally to real life.

The match between system and the real-world heuristic is consistent with two WCAG 2.0 standards:

- Guideline 3.1: Readable: Make text content readable and understandable.
- Guideline 3.2: Predictable: Make web pages appear and operate in predictable ways.

User Control and Freedom

Users often make mistakes and need clear exit paths but also need the freedom to decide they wanted to make that decision in the first place. For this heuristic, Nielsen recommends having easy access to undo and redo buttons.

The user control and freedom heuristic can be consistent with many accessibility standards. The specific point Nielsen is getting at, however, is the ability to move forward and backward within a page without losing content. This is consistent with one WCAG 2.0 accessibility standard:

- Guideline 3.3: Robust: Help users avoid and correct mistakes.

Consistency and Standards

This heuristic means that web designers should follow what users expect to see because it decreases the cognitive load on users. If users expect to see a library catalog called a "Library Catalog" but their library has changed it to "Find a Book," users may wonder if they can still find e-books and newspapers there. Consistency is key for users because they like familiarity.

The consistency and standards heuristics can be mapped to two WCAG 2.0 accessibility standards:

- Guideline 3.1: Readable: Make text content readable and understandable.
- Guideline 3.2: Predictable: Make web pages appear and operate in predictable ways.

Error Prevention

It's better to prevent a problem from developing in the first place than to craft a Pulitzer-worthy error message. Error messages are important, but it's more important to deconstruct those error messages to see if you can figure out how to redesign the web page to stop those errors from happening in the first place.

The error prevention heuristic maps to one WCAG 2.0 accessibility standard:

- Guideline 3.3: Robust: Help users avoid and correct mistakes.

Recognition Rather Than Recall

This usability heuristic means that it is less mentally taxing on users to see markers on the page that prompt them to recognize where they are on the website and how they got there than it does to make them remember. This is why it is a commonly accepted practice to place breadcrumb navigation on a web page, as a small reminder to users of where they are in the web page hierarchy.

The recognition rather than recall heuristic is consistent with one WCAG 2.0 accessibility standard:

- Guideline 2.4: Operable: Provide ways to help users navigate, find content, and determine where they are.

Flexibility and Efficiency of Use

The ability for a website to be flexible and to cater to different abilities of users is key to making it efficient for every user. Advanced users who come to a library website looking for advanced Boolean search filters will find it an effective and efficient search tool, as long as they know where those advanced search tools are. Novice, or beginner, searchers will find the basic search bar most efficient since they would likely be overwhelmed by the Boolean options of the advanced options. Efficiency is different for each person, so the ability of a website to personalize and flexibility for each user is important for the user experience. Relating to accessibility, it might be more efficient for a deaf user to read a video transcript than to sit through the time video captions.

The flexibility and efficiency of use heuristic is consistent with five WCAG 2.0 accessibility standards:

- Guideline 1.1: Perceivable: Provide text alternatives for any non-text content so that it can be changed into other forms people need, such as large print, braille, speech, symbols, or simpler language.
- Guideline 1.2: Perceivable: Provide alternatives for time-based media.
- Guideline 1.3: Perceivable: Create content that can be presented in different ways (for example simpler layout) without losing information or structure.
- Guideline 2.1: Operable: Make all functionality available from a keyboard.
- Guideline 4.1: Robust: Maximize compatibility with current and future user agents, including assistive technologies.

Aesthetic and Minimalist Design

Every piece of information on the web page matters. Too much takes away from the important pieces. If you have a popup dialogue box where you need to ask users if they are sure they want to place a hold on a library book, it is not as important that they need to know how many other users have the book on hold or how many other holds they have at the moment. Those pieces of information can be placed in unobtrusive ways so they don't interfere with the main task of the dialogue box—to place a hold or not. It also relates to the visual layout of the page—too much visual stimulation can overload the actual information on the page (e.g., the flashing rainbow web page backgrounds from the early 2000s).

The aesthetic and minimalist design heuristic is consistent with five WCAG 2.0 accessibility standards:

- Guideline 1.3: Perceivable: Create content that can be presented in different ways (for example simpler layout) without losing information or structure.
- Guideline 1.4 Perceivable: Make it easier for users to see and hear content including separating foreground from background.
- Guideline 2.2 Operable: Provide users enough time to read and use content.
- Guideline 2.3 Operable: Do not design content in a way that is known to cause seizures.
- Guideline 3.1 Understandable: Make text content readable and understandable.

Help Users Recognize, Diagnose, and Recover from Errors

Users should be able to understand exactly why the error happened, how to get back to the page they were on before, and how to prevent the error from happening the next time. This can include the text on error messages (which should include plain text instead of

REAL-LIFE SCENARIO

An example of the help and documentation heuristic in action, as well as giving users freedom via a library FAQ web page. It might say:

Q. How do I see online when my book is due back?
A. Click on My Account then click on Loans. The due date will show up next to each book title.

error codes that regular users wouldn't understand), but also suggestions for remediation—things to do next time to avoid the error message.

This usability heuristic is consistent with three WCAG 2.0 accessibility standards:

- Guideline 2.4: Operable: Provide ways to help users navigate, find content, and determine where they are.
- Guideline 3.2: Understandable: Make web pages appear and operate in predicable ways.
- Guideline 3.3: Understandable: Help users avoid and correct mistakes.

Help and Documentation

Every website should have some sort of user help or documentation to offer. While much of usability is to make it so the user won't need to access any help sites or help documentation, it is still a necessary piece of information to include as a part of websites.

These are most commonly found as FAQ web pages, where the help points that the web designer wanted to make are set out in the form of user questions and website designer answers on how to accomplish a specific task.

This usability heuristic is most consistent with one WCAG 2.0 accessibility guideline:

- Guideline 3.3: Understandable: Help users avoid and correct mistakes.

Seven Principles of Universal Design

Much like when we talked about the universal design for learning in chapter 8, this universal design is more holistic big picture than just thinking about how people learn. Universal design as a larger concept thinks about the different lives that people live and the differing means and methods they have for accessing information and solving problems. The seven principles of universal design are a broad framework by which to guide your thinking in any project—be it a website, a phone app, or even book kiosk (North Carolina State University 1997). Universal design, while applicable to websites and information technology in this book, applies to all projects in any aspect of library administration.

Principle 1: Equitable Use

The website needs to be able to be used by anyone regardless of their abilities or disabilities. Access should be seamless, and all users should have the same experience on the website. This principle includes several guidelines:

- Provide the same means of use for all users: identical whenever possible; equivalent when not.
- Avoid segregating or stigmatizing any users.
- Provisions for privacy, security, and safety should be equally available to all users.
- Make the design appealing to all users.

Principle 2: Flexibility in Use

The website needs to be able to be customized by users because we recognize that users come from a range of diverse backgrounds and have unique preferences. A truly universal website would be fully customizable, though it is not always technologically possible to offer such customizations. The best practice is to always offer as much customization as possible, and when in doubt, ask your users! This principle includes several guidelines:

- Provide choice in methods of use.
- Accommodate right- or left-handed access and use.
- Facilitate the user's accuracy and precision.
- Provide adaptability to the user's pace.

Principle 3: Simple and Intuitive Use

According to universal design, something should be simple and intuitive, regardless of the user's language or situation. Users shouldn't have to read a set of instructions to interact with the item (be it a website or a can opener); it should immediately be obvious what they should do. This principle includes several guidelines:

- Eliminate unnecessary complexity.
- Be consistent with user expectations and intuition.
- Accommodate a wide range of literacy and language skills.
- Arrange information consistent with its importance.
- Provide effective prompting and feedback during and after task completion.

Principle 4: Perceptible Information

This principle means that the information on the website needs to be understandable and comprehensible by the user, regardless of the user's abilities. This ties into writing accessible content by keeping in mind the reading level of your text as well as how you communicate that information to the user. Just because the information might be written in text, it doesn't have to be communicated to the user that way. Remember that users come with a variety of needs, abilities, and preferences, and try to make the information perceptible regardless of the method by which users choose to access the information. This principle includes several guidelines:

- Use different modes (pictorial, verbal, tactile) for redundant presentation of essential information.
- Provide adequate contrast between essential information and its surroundings.
- Maximize "legibility" of essential information.
- Differentiate elements in ways that can be described (i.e., make it easy to give instructions or directions).
- Provide compatibility with a variety of techniques or devices used by people with sensory limitations.

Principle 5: Tolerance for Error

It should be no surprise that people make a lot of mistakes. Librarians make mistakes, patrons make mistakes, and computer users make a lot of mistakes. It's easy to make mistakes on the computer. You don't pay attention to what you're typing for a second, and boom—you're on a 404 Page Not Found Error. One of the most important things you can do as a designer (of anything, including but not limited to websites) is to expect your users to make mistakes.

Once your product or website is complete, it's important to give it to a child or someone brand new who has no idea what to do with it and let that person mess around for a while and make mistakes. See what happens when those mistakes happen—are there error messages? Can the user back out of the error? Can he fix it? Is it something you can design out of the product entirely? Design into the product a tolerance and expectation for users to make mistakes. This principle includes several guidelines:

- Arrange elements to minimize hazards and errors: most used elements, most accessible; hazardous elements eliminated, isolated, or shielded.
- Provide warnings of hazards and errors.
- Provide fail safe features.
- Discourage unconscious action in tasks that require vigilance.

Principle 6: Low Physical Effort

If you are designing a product or website to fit within a universal design methodology, it is important to expect your users to not put in a lot of physical effort. This principle typically applies to physical products, like can openers, but just as easily can apply to websites as well. When you think about interaction design, do you imagine the user having to click on a lot of things or do a lot of dragging and dropping items around the screen? For a lower physical effort, consider quick clicks instead of drags. This principle includes several guidelines:

- Allow user to maintain a neutral body position.
- Use reasonable operating forces.
- Minimize repetitive actions.
- Minimize sustained physical effort.

Principle 7: Size and Space for Approach and Use

This principle seems solely for use with physical products, so you might like to think about it in terms of computer terminals in the library, and ensuring adequate space around each computer for all users, instead of having one computer for disabled use. But at a stretch, you could take it to mean size and space for use in website interactions—if a user needs to click on an icon, then the icon and the clickable area should both be big enough to easily click on and it also should be obvious where the clickable areas are. This principle includes several guidelines:

- Provide a clear line of sight to important elements for any seated or standing user.
- Make reach to all components comfortable for any seated or standing user.
- Accommodate variations in hand and grip size.
- Provide adequate space for the use of assistive devices or personal assistance.

The Person-Centered Approach

The person-centered approach began within the health professions, as a philosophy and methodology of interacting with patients. Pioneered by psychologist Carl Rogers between 1940 and 1960, it became a movement of self-actualization counseling therapy. There are still active person-centered approach therapy centers worldwide, and many health professions have taken aspects of Rogers's philosophy and integrated it into their own practice.

The modern person-centered approach (PCA) believes that people instinctually want to choose what's best for them, and the counselor, or mediator, is just there to act as a non-judgmental sounding board. It's more than just active listening, as it imposes a lot of rules on the mediator and requires many hours of training to become competent. The PCA uses a set of behaviors for both the patient and the counselor, acting in tandem.

Counselor/Librarian Behaviors

The counselor (or librarian, in this case) needs to have four behaviors, which in turn, engenders behaviors in the patient (or patron) (Lux, Motschnig-Pitrik, and Cornelius-White 2013, ch. 1). The counselor needs to exhibit:

- Non-directivity
- Empathy
- Congruence
- Unconditional positive regard

Non-directivity

The counselor, or person in charge of the session needs to be non-directive. This means that she cannot ask leading questions; she cannot have a set agenda or path she'd like the patient to take. She is there to facilitate, not to lead. This can take the form of many active listening traits, like rephrasing what you just heard, asking for clarification, making affirmative noises to let the speaker know you are listening, and non-directive body language (e.g., not shaking or nodding your head if they say something you didn't like).

This can relate to accessibility in many ways, but the most obvious is if you host a focus group or ask disabled people for their input on your library website. You will get the most effective feedback if you go into the session without an agenda, or potential solution in mind. Get the participants to start talking and let them lead the way.

Empathy

While this may seem to be a given, empathy is not something that comes easy to many people. Empathy is the ability to place yourself in someone else's shoes and to feel what that person might be feeling for yourself. Often confused with sympathy, empathy is not just a dispassionate pity for someone else's plight, but a visceral reaction because you can imagine what it feels like to be that other person.

When involving disabled people in a website accessibility or usability project, it is important to practice empathy beforehand, so you are not just another sympathetic face. Disabled people get a lot of sympathy from non-disabled people who have no idea what it is really like to live in a world that is designed to shut you out. Instead of empathy, they often get a pat on the head for "being an inspiration" or told to just deal with what they can get. Empathy is a vital tool to interact as human beings. It should be evident in your conversations with others but especially with those from oppressed and under-represented groups.

Congruence

Congruence is when all things are working toward the same end. In PCA, it means that both the counselor's words and the counselor's actions (her non-verbal behaviors) are in line with one another. Communication is a mixture of both verbal words and non-verbal cues. If you say one thing but your body language says something else, the person you are talking to will be confused or receive the wrong message. Congruence is the principle of being completely present and filled with positive regard for the patient, both with your words, but also with your non-verbal actions.

This can be difficult even for professional therapists because non-verbal actions are often unconscious actions. When faced with something that we don't like or are uncomfortable with, we might fold our arms in a defensive posture, shake our head no, purse our lips, narrow our eyes, or angle our shoulders away.

It takes a lot of practice and training to control our non-verbal cues during a conversation, but it is just as important as the actual words you say, again, especially when talking to groups of disabled people who are used to looking for any small sign of indifference or disgust. If you say something, then you must mean it with your actions as well.

Unconditional Positive Regard

Unconditional positive regard is not necessarily about "liking" the patient. You don't have to like others' personalities or life choices, but you must see their worth as a human being with an agency of their own and an innate self-determination for betterment. This, much like congruence, does not come easy. It is not easy to separate recognizing others' worth as human beings and their personalities or life choices. The "unconditional" caveat is hard too—no matter how poor my choices, I am still a human being with the possibility of improvement. That, in and of itself, was enough for Carl Rogers and PCA. That should be enough for librarians too.

It doesn't matter if disabled patrons actually use the library services, or what life choices they are making. They have worth as human beings—just as much worth as you, just as much worth as your non-disabled patrons. With unconditional positive regard, the possibility for self-attainment is within everyone, so there is no social stratification and no social pariahs. The feedback of a disabled patron counts just as much as a non-disabled patron.

Patient/Patron Behaviors

If the counselor communicates these emotions clearly and correctly, it will provide a safe space for the patient to experience the following:

- Actualizing tendency
- Primacy of experience
- Congruence

Actualizing Tendency

Many psychologists believe that we are born with an innate set of talents and possibilities and we naturally want to strive to meet our potentials. Abraham Maslow (of Maslow's triangle of needs) described self-actualized people as those who made "full use and exploitation of talents, capacities, potentialities, etc. Such people seem to be fulfilling themselves and to be doing the best that they are capable of doing" (Maslow 1954, 200).

The reason that PCA requires that counselors be non-directive is because if given a safe enough space and enough time, individuals will likely make decisions that lead toward their self-actualization—a release of their own talents, capacities, and potentialities.

When used in a library setting, it is important to remember that disabled people know their own talents and capacities much, much better than you do. If you follow a non-directive communication approach, and allow patrons to set the tone and cadence of the conversation, they will give you better answers and solutions to any website accessibility issue than you would come up with on your own.

Primacy of Experience

In PCA, the primacy of experience means that regardless of what a typical experience is, whatever someone experiences is valid for that person. It is a related field to phenomenology, but no two people experience something the exact same way. No two people experience driving a car the same way, just as no two people experience trying to access a website while disabled the same way. A complex web of past experience and current emotion combine to form two vastly different paths, yet both are entirely valid.

If you do any sort of focus groups, it is of the utmost importance to validate the experience of your users, even if you don't understand why, or you don't think it should have happened that way. A user experienced your website or library a certain way. That fact is immutable and you must go forward with that as an accepted fact.

Congruence

In a state of less fear and more trust where patients are more open to experiences and face themselves in a mindful way, they're more open to change in a positive direction. This

REAL-LIFE SCENARIO

A librarian was in a focus group of disabled patrons hoping to glean some information about the website, and one patron finally leaned forward and burst out, "You know what? I don't have website feedback right now, but I'm just frustrated because I wanted to get here for the makerspace class yesterday, but the cobblestones on the sidewalks are hell on my wrists and I was hurting too much to leave the house yesterday. You should be happy that I'm even here."

The librarian smiled sadly and replied, "It must be incredibly difficult to get around in a city that doesn't seem to care about how accessible its sidewalks are. I appreciate the difficulty you went through just to be here today to talk to me—are your wrists doing any better today? Is there any way that we could make the makerspace class a bit more accessible for you?"

freeing mind-set, and absence of fear or defensiveness, allows patients to begin to utilize their creativity to solve their own problems.

In a library setting, this congruence can be difficult to reach because it requires a level of trust between parties that a librarian and patron may rarely reach. If a librarian uses all the behaviors of PCA, though, it is more likely that the patrons will have less fear and less defensiveness, which will in turn lead to more fruitful problem solving and creative thinking.

In the sidebar exchange between a librarian and patron, the patron felt comfortable enough to express herself and her primacy of experience—what she experienced took precedence over everything else. The librarian exhibited empathy and unconditional positive regard—she never insulted the patron, ignored her, or pretended that her outburst didn't happen. The patron was treated with dignity and respect and non-directivity. Considering the focus group was about the library website, it could have been easy for the librarian to re-direct the conversation back to the website, but she continued the conversation about makerspaces because that is where the patron wanted to go. The person-centered approach, while used primarily in the health sciences, is a communication approach that is multidisciplinary and adaptable to nearly any situation.

Conclusion

If you've learned anything about all the "go back and do it again" language in this book, you've caught the gist of accessibility; it is not a one-time act. Accessibility is a process where you continually look for new standards and new ways to improve access to your website. It is also a state of mind; if you are not disabled, it takes practice and purposeful thinking to continually think about something that doesn't seem to directly benefit you.

If you find it difficult to keep thinking about accessibility, it's important to remember you have a duty of care as a librarian to provide access to information to all your patrons. If you read the beginning chapters on the many different types of disabilities and the assistive technologies that people use, you will know by now that disabilities are incredibly diverse. It is impossible to expect to make your website accessible to every patron with a visual disability because not all disabilities are the same.

Just as we appreciate diversity in our communities, families, and friends to bring in new points of view, lived experiences, and fresh perspectives, we can appreciate the diversity within the disabled community for what it is—a vibrant tapestry.

Just because link organization and clarity help disabled people and assistive technologies like screen readers, that doesn't mean that having organized links benefits only them. Smoothing out a sidewalk made of cobblestones or one that is full of cracks helps a mom pushing a baby stroller just as much as it helps disabled people. Similarly, an accessible website makes accessing information easier, smoother, and a much more pleasant experience for all patrons.

The ALA Code of Ethics (ALA 2006) places special emphasis on *equitable* access to information—not *equal* access. Equal access would be giving everyone the same website and it's unfortunate if they can't read or understand it, but they had just as much opportunity as everyone else. Equitable access, however, means that special care and effort is given to those who are under-privileged by society—whether through physical disability, mental illness, poverty, geography, or whatever form of disability it might be. Spending extra time and effort ensuring an accessible website gives your disabled patrons a more equitable chance to access information.

Accessing information is a fundamental human right. What we do with that information informs our very quality and nature of life. A researcher on deaf culture (Hintermair 2005) said that "individuals fashion new technologies and their applications in accordance with images of a life worth living." A life worth living is predicated on access to information, and it is our duty as librarians to help patrons access that information with whichever tools they use.

Key Points

This chapter covered some paths you can follow for further accessibility and usability once you've completed your website accessibility audits. Key points to remember:

- Usability heuristics are like rules of thumb—general principles to remember.
- Universal design looks holistically at a product and ensures its ease of use of everyone from first idea to final design.
- The person-centered approach is a method of communication that is commonly used in therapy that is non-directive, empathetic, positive, and congruent.
- The person-centered approach can be tailored to nearly any communication situation.
- Website accessibility benefits everyone.

Further Resources

- Shneiderman's Eight Golden Rules of Interface Design: https://www.cs.umd.edu/users/ben/goldenrules.html
- Don Norman's 7 Principles of Interaction Design: https://www.jnd.org/books/design-of-everyday-things-revised.html
- Tognazzini's First Principles of Interaction Design: http://asktog.com/atc/principles-of-interaction-design/

References

ALA (American Library Association). 2006. "Code of Ethics of the American Library Association." Advocacy, Legislation & Issues, July 7, 2006. http://www.ala.org/advocacy/proethics/codeofethics/codeethics.

Hintermair, Manfred. 2005. "Ethics, Deafness, and New Medical Technologies." *Journal of Deaf Studies and Deaf Education* 10 (2).

Lux, Michael, Renate Motschnig-Pitrik, and Jeffrey Cornelius-White. 2013. "The Essence of the Person-Centered Approach." In *Interdisciplinary Handbook of the Person-Centered Approach: Research and Theory*, 9–21. New York: Springer. https://doi.org/10.1007/978-1-4614-7141-7_2.

Maslow, Abraham. 1954. *Motivation and Personality.* 1st ed. New York: Harper & Row.

Nielsen, Jakob. 1995. "10 Usability Heuristics for User Interface Design." Nielsen-Norman Group. https://www.nngroup.com/articles/ten-usability-heuristics/.

North Carolina State University. 1997. "The Principles of Universal Design." Center for Universal Design. April 1, 1997. https://projects.ncsu.edu/ncsu/design/cud/about_ud/udprinciplestext.htm.

W3C. n.d. "Web Content Accessibility Guidelines (WCAG) 2.0." 2017. Accessed November 5, 2017. https://www.w3.org/TR/WCAG20/#meaning.

Appendix A
Sample Accessibility Testing Process

Rationale

The importance of accessibility in education today is unparalleled. Not only do state institutions need to provide proof of accessibility to even purchase a product, but many educational institutions run the risk of litigation if an e-learning object or course is not fully accessible. As the library is dedicated to academic, personal, and professional success for *all students*, it follows that we should be thought leaders in the realm of academic accessibility.

As librarians, it is our ethical and legal responsibility to ensure that our materials are accessible to students of all disabilities. This document is to provide a set process for testing our library website for accessibility, as well as guidance for how to analyze and report the testing results. To ensure consistent test situations, the test environment is provided as well as needed installations, and software or hardware requirements.

The testing process follows the WCAG 2.0 Four Principles of Accessibility:

1. Perceivable—Information and user interface components must be presentable to users in ways they can perceive.
   a. This means that users must be able to perceive the information being presented (it can't be invisible to all of their senses).
2. Operable—User interface components and navigation must be operable.
   a. This means that users must be able to operate the interface (the interface cannot require interaction that a user cannot perform).
3. Understandable—Information and the operation of user interface must be understandable.
   a. This means that users must be able to understand the information as well as the operation of the user interface (the content or operation cannot be beyond their understanding).

4. Robust—Content must be robust enough that it can be interpreted reliably by a wide variety of user agents, including assistive technologies.
    a. This means that users must be able to access the content as technologies advance (as technologies and user agents evolve, the content should remain accessible).

For each of these principles, there will be testing tasks that correspond with each of the sub-guidelines of each principle. Under the "Test Process" section, normative standards and minimum compliance, along with recommended actions to be taken, will be provided.

Test Environment

Recommended software:

- Color Contrast Analyzer—Download for Mac/Windows
- Readability Test Tool—Bookmark
- Screen Reader—VoiceOver for Mac/iOS (found under preferences → Accessibility), and NVDA or JAWS for Windows
- Web Accessibility Check (Use one of the following)
    - WAVE Accessibility Tool
    - CodeSniffer
    - Functional Accessibility Evaluator
    - Photosensitive Epilepsy Analysis Tool

Please test in both Windows and Mac environments, if possible. If not, one environment will suffice.

Test Process

Principle 1: Perceivable—Information and User Interface Components Must be Presentable to Users in Ways They Can Perceive

Guideline 1.1 Text Alternatives: Provide text alternatives for any non-text content so that it can be changed into other forms people need, such as large print, braille, speech, symbols or simpler language.

- Task 1.1.1: Run the page through one of the web checkers (WAVE or CodeSniffer) to identify any missing alternative image text. If images or other non-text media are unnecessary to the content, ensure they are implemented in a way that can be ignored by assistive technology (e.g., "null").
- Task 1.1.2: Verify that media (audio or video) is also offered in a text/transcript format.
- Task 1.1.3: If there are interactive elements reliant upon one of the senses (hover-over, color change, etc.), the information must be provided in an alternate method.

Guideline 1.2 Time-Based Media: Provide alternatives for time-based media.

- Task 1.2.1: The transcript of video or audio must be offered both in a synchronized (closed captions) option as well as an unsynchronized (text-only) option.
- Task 1.2.2: If something is time limited, the user must be given warnings about how much time is remaining—audio and visual warnings.

Guideline 1.3 Adaptable: Create content that can be presented in different ways (for example, different layout) without losing information or structure.

- Task 1.3.1: In the browser, disable the style sheet to ensure the content is still logical.
- Task 1.3.2: Does a screen reader navigate the content in a logical order?
- Task 1.3.3: Does the screen reader have the option of skipping unnecessary navigation links?

Guideline 1.4 Distinguishable: Make it easier for users to see and hear content including separating foreground from background.

- Task 1.4.1: Use the Color Analyzer to ensure that the foreground-text-to-background-color ratio is at least 4.5:1. Ideally, it will be greater than 6:1.

Table A.1.

FAILURE CONDITION	COMPLIANCE	NON-COMPLIANCE
Task 1.1.1: The web-check results show missing alt tags.	All images have an alt tag, and if they are not relevant to the content, they are skipped (e.g., "null," or "image of library website homepage").	Images have no tag or unhelpful tags that provide no relevant information (e.g., "img12").
Task 1.1.2: Videos do not offer captions or a transcript.	All media is provided in an opt-in transcript format (e.g., closed captions and/or "Read Transcript" link).	There are limited options for transcripts or they are not available.
Task 1.1.3: Interactive elements (e.g., hover-overs, sliders) are not accessible via other means.	Elements that rely upon one sense are also offered in an alternate method (e.g., hover-overs are also included in a transcript, or color changes are also noted by text).	Elements that rely on one sense are not available in an alternate method.
Task 1.2.1: Videos only offer CCs but no option for anything non-synchronized.	Videos (and other timed media) must offer non-synchronized.	Videos (and other timed media) only offer the synchronized option.
Task 1.2.2: Timed quizzes do not give warnings about time remaining.	Timed items must give enough warning about how much time remains.	Timed items do not give any or insufficient warning about time remaining.
Task 1.3.1: If the style sheet is disabled, the website is unnavigable.	The website must follow a logical order when CSS is disabled.	The website is un-navigable if the CSS is disabled.

(continued)

Table A.1. *(Continued)*

FAILURE CONDITION	COMPLIANCE	NON-COMPLIANCE
Task 1.3.2: The screen reader doesn't read the website in a logical order.	Everything is ordered and read in the logical order.	The screen reader does not follow the flow of the website.
Task 1.3.3: The screen reader always reads unnecessary navigation links.	The user can skip unnecessary navigation links (e.g., "skip to content").	The user cannot skip the navigation links.
Task 1.4.1: The colors (foreground : background) are not within the correct ratio.	The color ratio is greater than 4.5:1.	The color ratio is less than 4.5:1.

Principle 2: Operable—User Interface Components and Navigation Must be Operable

Guideline 2.1 Keyboard Accessible: Make all functionality available from a keyboard.

- Task 2.1.1: Can you navigate the site using only the keyboard? Do you get stuck in any keyboard traps where you cannot get out?
- Task 2.1.2: Are any forms or interactivities able to be accessed via keyboard?

Guideline 2.2 Enough Time: Provide enough time for users to read and use content.

- Task 2.2.1: If anything is time based (text on videos or tutorials, quizzes), are users able to stop the timer to read the content or somehow get more time?

Guideline 2.3 Seizures: Do not design content in a way that is known to cause seizures.

- Task 2.3.1: Perform a periodic check for the site on the Photosensitive Epilepsy Analysis Tool

Guideline 2.4 Navigable: Find ways to help users navigate, find content, and determine where they are.

- Task 2.4.1: If there are repeated blocks of links (like navigation links), are these skippable (e.g., does the screen reader skip them?)
- Task 2.4.2: Is the navigation sequential? Does it go in a logical order?

Table A.2.

FAILURE CONDITION	COMPLIANCE	NON-COMPLIANCE
Task 2.1.1: The page cannot be navigated via keyboard.	Everything can be navigated and used via keyboard.	The user gets stuck or cannot progress via keyboard.
Task 2.1.2: The forms are not able to be used via keyboard only.	The forms can be used via only the keyboard.	The forms cannot be used by the keyboard.

FAILURE CONDITION	COMPLIANCE	NON-COMPLIANCE
Task 2.2.1: For timed material, the user cannot stop the material to get more time.	For timed material, the user can stop the timer to have enough time to complete the material.	For timed material, the user cannot stop the timer.
Task 2.3.1: An item flashes three or more times in one second.	Nothing flashes three or more times per second.	Items flash three or more times in one second.
Task: 2.4.1: The screen reader repeatedly reads navigation links.	The screen reader and user can skip repeated navigation links.	The screen reader and user cannot skip repeated navigation links.
Task 2.4.2: The content is not read in a logical order.	The content is read in a logical order.	The content is not read in a logical order.

Principle 3: Understandable—Information and the Operation of the User Interface Must be Understandable

Guideline 3.1 Readable: Make text content readable and understandable.

- Task 3.1.1: Can the page be automatically translated into another language?

Guideline 3.2 Predictable: Make web pages appear and operate in predictable ways.

- Task 3.2.1: Does the site change without the user able to stop it?

Guideline 3.3 Input Assistance: Helps users avoid and correct mistakes.

- Task 3.3.1: If an error is made in a text-entry field, does it let the user know?
- Task 3.3.2: If text entry is required, are there labels to let the user know what is required?

Table A.3.

FAILURE CONDITION	COMPLIANCE	NON-COMPLIANCE
Task 3.1.1: The page cannot be translated into any language other than English.	The page can be translated into another language.	The page cannot be translated into any other language.
Task 3.2.1: The site changes on its own.	The user makes any change happen.	The site changes on its own.
Task 3.3.1: Nothing lets the user know about errors in the text-entry field.	Users are notified about any text-entry errors and given a chance to correct them.	Users are not notified about any text-entry errors or given a chance to correct them.
Task 3.3.2: There are no labels about what is required for text-entry fields.	Every text-entry field is labeled about what is required.	Text-entry fields are not labeled about what is required.

Principle 4: Robust—Content Must be Robust Enough That It Can Be Interpreted Reliably by a Wide Variety of User Agents, Including Assistive Technologies

Guideline 4.1 Compatible: Maximize compatibility with current and future user agents, including assistive technologies.

- Task 4.1.1: Is the code clean? Are there any hanging tags or errors in the code?

Table A.4.

FAILURE CONDITION	COMPLIANCE	NON-COMPLIANCE
Task 4.1.1: The code has errors.	The code is standards compliant.	The code is not standards compliant.

Test Reporting and Analysis

- Copy and complete an Accessibility Testing Report.
- Make needed changes.
- Update the Accessibility Statement on the library website.

Appendix B

Accessibility Testing Report

Table B.1.

TESTER:	DATE:		TESTING URL:	TESTING ENVIRONMENT NOTES:
WCAG GUIDELINE	TASK	PASS/FAIL	ACTION ITEM	NOTES
Guideline 1	1.1.1			
	1.1.2			
	1.1.3			
	1.2.1			
	1.2.2			
	1.3.1			
	1.3.2			
	1.3.3			
	1.4.1			
Guideline 2	2.1.1			
	2.1.2			
	2.2.1			
	2.3.1			
	2.4.1			
	2.4.2			
Guideline 3	3.1.1			
	3.2.1			
	3.3.1			
	3.3.2			
Guideline 4	4.1.1			

Bibliography

Able Player. "Able Player." Accessed April 4, 2017. https://ableplayer.github.io/ableplayer/.

———. "Able Player Audio Demo #4." Able Player. Accessed August 8, 2017. http://ableplayer.github.io/ableplayer/demos/audio4.html.

———. "Able Player Examples." Accessed August 8, 2017. http://ableplayer.github.io/ableplayer/demos/index.html.

Accessibility and Usability at Penn State. "Font Face." Accessed April 30, 2017. http://accessibility.psu.edu/legibility/fontface/.

———. "Image ALT Tag Tips for HTML." Accessed March 26, 2017. http://accessibility.psu.edu/images/imageshtml/.

"ADA Amendments Act of 2008." September 25, 2008. https://www.gpo.gov/fdsys/pkg/PLAW-110publ325/html/PLAW-110publ325.htm.

Adams, Mike. *Towards Inclusive Learning in Higher Education: Developing Curricula for Disabled Students*. New York: Routledge, 2009.

AFB (American Foundation for the Blind). "Accessible Video Player, Version 1.1." Accessed August 8, 2017. http://www.afb.org/info/programs-and-services/technology-evaluation/creating-accessible-websites/download-afbs-accessible-html5-video-player/1235.

———. "Refreshable Braille Displays." Accessed March 26, 2017. http://www.afb.org/prodBrowseCatResults.aspx?CatID=43.

———. "Screen Reader Tips for Using the Web." Accessed March 26, 2017. http://www.afb.org/info/programs-and-services/daily-living/afb-senior-site-etips/see-all-featured-etips/screen-reader-tips-for-using-the-web/12345.

ALA (American Library Association). "Access." Accessed May 7, 2017. http://www.ala.org/advocacy/access.

———. "Advocacy University." Accessed May 7, 2017. http://www.ala.org/advocacy/advocacy-university.

———. "Code of Ethics of the American Library Association." Advocacy, Legislation & Issues. July 7, 2006. http://www.ala.org/advocacy/proethics/codeofethics/codeethics.

Alexander, Larry, and Michael Moore. "Deontological Ethics." In *The Stanford Encyclopedia of Philosophy*, edited by Edward N. Zalta, winter 2016. Metaphysics Research Lab, Stanford University, 2016. https://plato.stanford.edu/archives/win2016/entries/ethics-deontological/.

Alzheimer's Association. "Latest Facts & Figures Report." 2017. Accessed May 18, 2017. https://www.alz.org/facts/overview.asp.

American Academy of Ophthalmology. "Computers, Digital Devices and Eye Strain." March 1, 2016. Accessed March 26, 2017. https://www.aao.org/eye-health/tips-prevention/computer-usage.

American Dyslexia Association. "About Dyslexia." Accessed May 18, 2017. http://www.american-dyslexia-association.com/Dyslexia.html.

Badarudeen, Sameer, and Sanjeev Sabharwal. "Assessing Readability of Patient Education Materials: Current Role in Orthopaedics." *Clinical Orthopaedics and Related Research* 468, no. 10 (October 2010): 2572–80. https://doi.org/10.1007/s11999-010-1380-y.

Ballav, Alipta. "Mental Models and User Experience: UXmatters." UX Matters, May 17, 2016. http://www.uxmatters.com/mt/archives/2016/05/mental-models-and-user-experience.php.

Barnes, Marian. *Care in Everyday Life: An Ethic of Care in Practice*. Bristol, UK: Policy, 2012. https://doi.org/10.1332/policypress/9781847428233.001.0001.

BBC. "Data, Information and Knowledge." Accessed November 12, 2017. https://www.bbc.co.uk/education/guides/zkfbkqt/revision/2.

Boedy, Matthew. "From Deliberation to Responsibility: Ethics, Invention, and Bonhoeffer in Technical Communication." *Technical Communication Quarterly* 26, no. 2 (April 3, 2017): 116–26. https://doi.org/10.1080/10572252.2017.1287309.

"British Deaf Association—Home." Accessed April 15, 2017. https://bda.org.uk/.

Brownstein, Michael, and Jennifer Saul, eds. *Implicit Bias and Philosophy, Volume 2: Moral Responsibility, Structural Injustice, and Ethics*. Oxford: Oxford University Press, 2016. https://doi.org/10.1093/acprof:oso/9780198766179.001.0001.

Bruce, Susan, Catherine Nelson, Angel Perez, Brent Stutzman, and Brooke A. Barnhill. "The State of Research on Communication and Literacy in Deafblindness." *American Annals of the Deaf* 161, no. 4 (2016): 424–43.

Card, Claudia. "Responsibility Ethics, Shared Understandings, and Moral Communities." *Hypatia* 17, no. 1 (2002): 141–55. https://doi.org/10.1111/j.1527-2001.2002.tb00684.x.

Carel, Havi. "Why Use Phenomenology to Study Illness?" In *Phenomenology of Illness*. Oxford: Oxford University Press, 2016. https://doi.org/10.1093/acprof:oso/9780199669653.003.0002.

Carlson, Jerry S., and Karl Heinz Wiedl. "Principles of Dynamic Assessment: The Application of a Specific Model." *Learning and Individual Differences* 4, no. 2 (1992): 153–66. https://doi.org/10.1016/1041-6080(92)90011-3.

CAST. "About Universal Design for Learning." Accessed May 11, 2017. http://www.cast.org/our-work/about-udl.html#.WRSbVFXyuUl.

CDC (Centers for Disease Control and Prevention). "Key Findings: Prevalence of Disability and Disability Type among Adults, United States—2013." Disability and Health. August 20, 2015. https://www.cdc.gov/ncbddd/disabilityandhealth/features/key-findings-community-prevalence.html.

Center for Community Health and Development. "Assessing Community Needs and Resources." Community Toolbox. Accessed August 1, 2017. http://ctb.ku.edu/en/table-of-contents/assessment/assessing-community-needs-and-resources/conduct-focus-groups/main.

Center for History and New Media. "Zotero Quick Start Guide." n.d. Accessed June 3, 2017. http://zotero.org/support/quick_start_guide.

Centre for Excellence in Universal Design. "The 7 Principles." What Is Universal Design. Accessed November 8, 2017. http://universaldesign.ie/What-is-Universal-Design/The-7-Principles/.

Colorado State University. "Creating a Video Transcript: The ACCESS Project." Accessed March 26, 2017. http://accessproject.colostate.edu/udl/modules/multimedia/tut_video_transcript.php.

Constantin, Eugen. "Deontology in Public Administration." *Contemporary Readings in Law and Social Justice* 6 (2014): 432–36.

"Contact Sky Using British Sign Language—Sky Accessibility." Accessed April 15, 2017. https://accessibility.sky.com/contact-us/contact-sky-using-british-sign-language.

DAISY Consortium. "DAISY Technology." 2017. http://www.daisy.org/daisy-technology.

Dalrymple, Theodore. "The Inverse Care Law." *BMJ* 344 (March 7, 2012). https://doi.org/10.1136/bmj.e1633.

Dave, Anish. "Categories as Rhetorical Barriers and the Federal Response to Hurricane Katrina." *Technical Communication Quarterly* 24, no. 3 (July 3, 2015): 258–86. https://doi.org/10.1080/10572252.2015.1044121.

Dean, M. R., and H. J. McDermott. "Preferred Listening Levels: The Effect of Background Noise for Moderate-to-Profoundly Hearing Impaired Aid Users." *Scandinavian Audiology* 29, no. 3 (August 8, 2000): 139–49.

Digital Equity for Learning. 2016. http://digitalequityforlearning.org/.

Donnison, David. "Looking Ahead." In *Speaking to Power*, 145–58. Bristol, UK: Policy, 2009. https://doi.org/10.1332/policypress/9781847420381.003.0011.

Enns, Charlotte. "Critical Literacy: Deaf Adults Speak Out." *Exceptionality Education International* 19 (2009): 3–20. http://ir.lib.uwo.ca/eei/vol19/iss2/2.

Environmental Protection Agency. "Public Participation Guide: Selecting the Right Level of Public Participation." International Cooperation. Accessed August 1, 2017. https://www.epa.gov/international-cooperation/public-participation-guide-selecting-right-level-public-participation.

Epilepsy.org. "Photosensitive Epilepsy." March 2015. https://www.epilepsy.org.uk/info/photosensitive-epilepsy.

"Equality Act 2010." Legislation, 2010. http://www.legislation.gov.uk/ukpga/2010/15/part/6/chapter/2.

"Equality-in-HE-Statistical-Report-2015-Part-2-Students.pdf." Accessed April 23, 2017. http://www.ecu.ac.uk/wp-content/uploads/2015/11/Equality-in-HE-statistical-report-2015-part-2-students.pdf.

Equal Opportunity for Individuals with Disabilities, 42 U.S. Code § Chapter 126 (1990). https://www.law.cornell.edu/uscode/text/42/12101.

Feest, Uljana. "Historical Perspectives on Erklären and Verstehen: Introduction." In *Historical Perspectives on Erklären and Verstehen*, edited by Uljana Feest, 21:1–13. Dordrecht: Springer Netherlands, 2010. https://doi.org/10.1007/978-90-481-3540-0_1.

"Findings and Purposes of ADA Amendments Act of 2008." The Americans with Disabilities Act of 1990, as Amended, 2009. https://www.ada.gov/pubs/adastatute08markscrdr.htm#12101note.

Fletcher, Howard. "The Principles of Inclusive Design: They Include You." 2006. http://www.designcouncil.org.uk/sites/default/files/asset/document/the-principles-of-inclusive-design.pdf.

Freire, Paulo. *Pedagogy of the Oppressed.* Translated by Myra Bergman Ramos. 2nd rev. ed. London: Penguin, 1996.

Frid, Linnea, Alvaro García, Iker Laskibar, Aitziber Etxaniz, and Mari Feli Gonzalez. "What Technology Can and Cannot Offer an Ageing Population: Current Situation and Future Approach." In *A Multimodal End-2-End Approach to Accessible Computing*, edited by Pradipta Biswas and Carlos Duarte, 3–22. London: Springer, 2015. https://doi.org/10.1007/978-1-4471-6708-2_1.

Gannon-Leary, Pat, and Michael D. McCarthy. "Questioning and Active Listening." In *Customer Care*, 83–99. Oxford, UK: Chandos, 2010. https://doi.org/10.1016/B978-1-84334-570-1.50006-1.

GitHub. "Ableplayer/Ableplayer: Fully Accessible Cross-Browser HTML5 Media Player." Accessed March 26, 2017. https://github.com/ableplayer/ableplayer.

González, María de la O, Francisco Jareño, and Raquel López. "Impact of Students' Behavior on Continuous Assessment in Higher Education." *Innovation: The European Journal of Social Science Research* 28, no. 4 (October 2, 2015): 498–507. https://doi.org/10.1080/13511610.2015.1060882.

GSA Government-wide Section 508 Accessibility Program. "Section 508 Law and Related Laws and Policies." Section508.gov, n.d. https://www.section508.gov/content/learn/laws-and-policies.

Hanna, Kathleen A., Mindy M. Cooper, and Robin A. Crumrin. "Introduction to Diversity in Academic Libraries." In *Diversity Programming and Outreach for Academic Libraries*, 1–15. Oxford, UK: Chandos, 2011. https://doi.org/10.1016/B978-1-84334-635-7.50001-4.

Hearing Loss Association of North Carolina. "Captions Definition." Accessed March 26, 2017. http://www.nchearingloss.org/caption.htm.

Higher Education Statistics Agency. "Widening Participation Summary: UK Performance Indicators 2015/16." February 2017. https://www.hesa.ac.uk/data-and-analysis/performance-indicators/widening-participation-summary.

Hill, Thomas E. "Kantian Autonomy and Contemporary Ideas of Autonomy." In *Kant on Moral Autonomy*, edited by Oliver Sensen. Cambridge: Cambridge University Press, 2012. https://doi.org/10.1017/CBO9780511792489.003.

Hintermair, Manfred. "Ethics, Deafness, and New Medical Technologies." *Journal of Deaf Studies and Deaf Education* 10, no. 2 (2005).

Idea Sandbox. "Better Problem Solving with Framing." Accessed July 25, 2017. https://idea-sandbox.com/blog/frame-your-problems-to-create-better-solutions/.

"JAWS Screen Reader—Best in Class." Accessed March 26, 2017. http://www.freedomscientific.com/Products/Blindness/JAWS.

JISC. "Inclusive Assessment." Transforming Assessment and Feedback with Technology. 2016. https://www.jisc.ac.uk/guides/transforming-assessment-and-feedback/inclusive-assessment.

Kalyuga, Slava. *Rapid Dynamic Assessment for Learning. Vol. 18. Education in the Asia-Pacific Region: Issues, Concerns and Prospects.* Dordrecht: Springer Science+Business Media, 2012.

Knauf, Helen. "Reading, Listening and Feeling: Audio Feedback as a Component of an Inclusive Learning Culture at Universities." *Assessment & Evaluation in Higher Education* 41, no. 3 (April 2, 2016): 442–49. https://doi.org/10.1080/02602938.2015.1021664.

Kushalnagar, Poorna, Joan Naturale, Raylene Paludneviciene, Scott R. Smith, Emily Werfel, Richard Doolittle, Stephen Jacobs, and James DeCaro. "Health Websites: Accessibility and Usability for American Sign Language Users." *Health Communication* 30, no. 8 (2015): 830–37. https://doi.org/10.1080/10410236.2013.853226.

Kuttner, Paul. "The Problem with That Equity vs. Equality Graphic You're Using." Cultural Organizing. 2015. http://culturalorganizing.org/the-problem-with-that-equity-vs-equality-graphic/.

Lam, Catherine G., Debra L. Roter, and Kenneth J. Cohen. "Survey of Quality, Readability, and Social Reach of Websites on Osteosarcoma in Adolescents." *Patient Education and Counseling* 90, no. 1 (January 2013): 82–87. https://doi.org/10.1016/j.pec.2012.08.006.

Laplante-Lévesque, Ariane, M. Kathleen Pichora-Fuller, and Jean-Pierre Gagné. "Providing an Internet-Based Audiological Counselling Programme to New Hearing Aid Users: A Qualitative Study." *International Journal of Audiology* 45, no. 12 (January 1, 2006): 697–706. https://doi.org/10.1080/14992020600944408.

Leigh, Irene W. *A Lens on Deaf Identities*. Oxford: Oxford University Press, 2009. https://doi.org/10.1093/acprof:oso/9780195320664.001.0001.

Limentani, Alexander. "The Role of Ethical Principles in Health Care and the Implications for Ethical Codes." *Journal of Medical Ethics* 25 (n.d.). Accessed April 15, 2017.

Lux, Michael, Renate Motschnig-Pitrik, and Jeffrey Cornelius-White. "The Essence of the Person-Centered Approach." In *Interdisciplinary Handbook of the Person-Centered Approach: Research and Theory*, 9–21. New York: Springer New York, 2013. https://doi.org/10.1007/978-1-4614-7141-7_2.

Marom, Amnon. "Universality, Particularity, and Potentiality: The Sources of Human Divergence as Arise from Wilhelm Dilthey's Writings." *Human Studies* 37, no. 1 (June 2014): 1–13.

Maslow, Abraham. *Motivation and Personality*. 1st ed. New York: Harper & Row, 1954.

McGraw, Harold. "SMOG Formula." Accessed May 14, 2017. http://library.med.utah.edu/Patient_Ed/workshop/handouts/smog_formula.pdf.

McKeown, Anthony. *Overcoming Information Poverty*. San Diego, CA: Elsevier Science, 2016.

Merriam-Webster. S.v. "Advocacy." Accessed July 25, 2017. https://www.merriam-webster.com/dictionary/advocacy.

———. S.v. "Express." Accessed May 11, 2017. https://www.merriam-webster.com/dictionary/express.

Microsoft. "Enable Readability Statistics." Test Your Document's Readability. 2016. https://support.office.com/en-ie/article/Test-your-document-s-readability-85b4969e-e80a-4777-8dd3-f7fc3c8b3fd2?ui=en-US&rs=en-IE&ad=IE.

———. "Kinect—Windows App Development." Accessed April 15, 2017. https://developer.microsoft.com/en-us/windows/kinect.

Moorcroft, Heather. "Libraries as Sites for Contested Knowledges: Collection Development in the Area of Aboriginal Studies." *Collection Building* 16, no. 3 (September 1, 1997): 108–12. https://doi.org/10.1108/01604959710172387.

Moreno, Susan, and Carol O'Neal. "Tips for Teaching High-Functioning People with Autism." Indiana Resource Center for Autism. 2000. https://www.iidc.indiana.edu/pages/Tips-for-Teaching-High-Functioning-People-with-Autism.

Mozilla Developer Network. "An Overview of Accessible Web Applications and Widgets." March 13, 2017. https://developer.mozilla.org/en-US/docs/Web/Accessibility/An_overview_of_accessible_web_applications_and_widgets.

Mykitiuk, R., A. Chaplick, and C. Rice. "Beyond Normative Ethics: Ethics of Arts-Based Disability Research." *Ethics, Medicine and Public Health* 1, no. 3 (July 2015): 373–82. https://doi.org/10.1016/j.jemep.2015.07.005.

National Association of the Deaf. "President Updates, March 2017." National Association of the Deaf—NAD. 2017. https://www.nad.org/2017/03/27/president-updates-march-2017/.

National Center for Education Statistics. "Demographics—Overall." *National Assessment of Adult Literacy.* Accessed April 30, 2017. https://nces.ed.gov/naal/kf_demographics.asp.

National Center on Deaf-Blindness. "Overview on Deaf-Blindness." October 1, 2008. Accessed May 14, 2017. https://nationaldb.org/library/page/1934.

National Center on Universal Design for Learning. "Principle I. Provide Multiple Means of Representation." Last updated March 7, 2014. Accessed May 7, 2017. http://www.udlcenter.org/aboutudl/udlguidelines/principle1.

———. "Principle III. Provide Multiple Means of Engagement." Last updated March 7, 2014. Accessed May 11, 2017. http://www.udlcenter.org/aboutudl/udlguidelines/principle3.

———. "What Is Universal Design for Learning?" Accessed May 7, 2017. http://www.udlcenter.org/aboutudl/whatisudl.

National Eye Institute. "Facts about Color Blindness." National Institutes of Health. n.d. https://nei.nih.gov/health/color_blindness/facts_about.

Newell, Alan F. "Design and the Digital Divide: Insights from 40 Years in Computer Support for Older and Disabled People." *Synthesis Lectures on Assistive, Rehabilitative, and Health-Preserving Technologies* 1, no. 1 (June 28, 2011): 1–195. https://doi.org/10.2200/S00369ED1V01Y201106ARH001.

Nielsen, Jakob. "10 Usability Heuristics for User Interface Design." Nielsen-Norman Group. 1995. https://www.nngroup.com/articles/ten-usability-heuristics/.

North, Marjorie. "Mastering the Basics of Communication." Harvard Division of Continuing Education. 2016. https://www.extension.harvard.edu/professional-development/blog/mastering-basics-communication.

North Carolina State University. "The Principles of Universal Design." Center for Universal Design. April 1, 1997. https://projects.ncsu.edu/ncsu/design/cud/about_ud/udprinciplestext.htm.

Office of Information and Regulatory Affairs. "Nondiscrimination on the Basis of Disability; Accessibility of Web Information and Services of Public Accommodations." Spring 2015. https://www.reginfo.gov/public/do/eAgendaViewRule?pubId=201504&RIN=1190-AA61.

Oregon State University. "Alternative Text for Images." Accessed March 26, 2017. http://oregonstate.edu/accessibility/alttext.

Origin Instruments. "Sip and Puff Switch Solutions." Accessed 2017. http://www.orin.com/.

"OzPlayer—AccessibilityOz." Accessed August 8, 2017. https://www.accessibilityoz.com/ozplayer/.

PedRIO with Plymouth University. "Inclusive Assessment." Accessed April 6, 2017. https://www1.plymouth.ac.uk/research/pedrio/Documents/PedRIO%20Paper%207.pdf.

Peterson, Clarissa. *Learning Responsive Web Design*. Sebastopol, Canada: O'Reilly, 2014.

Pew Research Center. "Demographics of Mobile Device Ownership and Adoption in the United States." 2016. http://www.pewinternet.org/fact-sheet/mobile/.

Pipes, Alan. *How to Design Websites*. London: Laurence King, 2011.

Prakash, Aseem Gugerty, and Mary Kay. *Advocacy Organizations and Collective Actions*. Cambridge: Cambridge University Press, 2011.

"Projects/Orca—GNOME Wiki!" Accessed March 26, 2017. https://wiki.gnome.org/Projects/Orca.

Quaker.org. "Speak Truth to Power." Originally published March 2, 1955. http://www.quaker.org/sttp.html.

Quality Assurance Agency. "Quality Code Part B." Assuring and Enhancing Academic Quality. January 1, 2014. http://www.qaa.ac.uk/assuring-standards-and-quality/the-quality-code/quality-code-part-b.

Republic of South Africa. *White Paper for Social Welfare*. Department of Welfare. August 1997. Accessed April 16, 2017. http://www.gov.za/sites/www.gov.za/files/White_Paper_on_Social_Welfare_0.pdf.

Riddell, Sheila, and Elisabet Weedon. "Disabled Students in Higher Education: Discourses of Disability and the Negotiation of Identity." *Special Issues: Representing Diversity in Education: Student Identities in Contexts of Learning and Instruction & Classroom-Based Talk* 63 (2014): 38–46. https://doi.org/10.1016/j.ijer.2013.02.008.

Roberts, Joanne. "From Know-How to Show-How? Questioning the Role of Information and Communication Technologies in Knowledge Transfer." *Technology Analysis & Strategic Management* 12, no. 4 (December 1, 2000): 429–43. https://doi.org/10.1080/713698499.

Salvo, Michael J. "Ethics of Engagement: User-Centered Design and Rhetorical Methodology." *Technical Communication Quarterly* 10, no. 3 (July 1, 2001): 273–90. https://doi.org/10.1207/s15427625tcq1003_3.

Savitch, Nada, and Panayiotis Zaphiris. *Accessible Websites for People with Dementia: A Preliminary Investigation Info Information Architecture*. Berlin: Springer-Verlag, 2006. http://innovationsindementia.org.uk/publications/ICCHP_NSavitch.pdf.

Scheffran, Jürgen. "Tools for Stakeholder Assessment and Interaction." In *Stakeholder Dialogues in Natural Resources Management: Theory and Practice*, edited by Susanne Stollkleemann and Martin Welp, 153–85. Berlin, Heidelberg: Springer Berlin Heidelberg, 2006. https://doi.org/10.1007/978-3-540-36917-2_6.

"Screen Readers and Screen Magnifiers: An Introduction to Computer Accessibility Software." n.d. Accessed March 30, 2017. http://www.afb.org/info/living-with-vision-loss/using-technology/using-a-computer/part-ii-for-the-experienced-computer-user-with-a-new-visual-impairment/screen-readers-and-screen-magnifiers/12345.

"Sections 501 and 505 of the Rehabilitation Act of 1973." Accessed March 30, 2017. https://www.eeoc.gov/laws/statutes/rehab.cfm.

Shahrazad, Hadad. "Knowledge Economy: Characteristics and Dimensions." *Management Dynamics in the Knowledge Economy* 5, no. 2 (2017): 203–25.

Sher, George. "Responsibility and Practical Reason." In *Action, Ethics, and Responsibility*, edited by Joseph Keim Campbell, Michael O'Rourke, and Harry S. Silverstein, 203–18. Cambridge, MA: MIT Press, 2010. https://doi.org/10.7551/mitpress/9780262014731.003.0011.

SignVideo. "British Sign Language Video Interpreting Services." Accessed April 15, 2017. http://www.signvideo.co.uk/.

Simpson, Eleanor H., and Peter D. Balsam. "The Behavioral Neuroscience of Motivation: An Overview of Concepts, Measures, and Translational Applications." In *Behavioral Neuroscience of Motivation*, 1–12. Cham, Switzerland: Springer International, 2016. https://doi.org/10.1007/7854_2015_402.

Siple, Linda, Leslie Greer, and Barbara Ray Holcomb. "Deaf Culture Tip Sheet." 2004. https://www.rit.edu/ntid/radscc/sites/rit.edu.ntid.radscc/files/file_attachments/deaf_culture_tip_sheet.pdf.

Stringer, Dan. "Keyboard Traps." *Humanising Technology Blog*. April 13, 2011. https://www.nomensa.com/blog/2011/keyboard-traps.

Sutherland, Andrew. "Time to Celebrate Neurodiversity in the Workplace." *Occupational Health* 68, no. 11 (November 2016): 11.

TeachICT. "Foot Control." Accessed May 20, 2017. http://www.teach-ict.com/gcse_new/computer%20systems/disability_accessibility/miniweb/pg3.htm.

Tillery, Denise. "Power, Language, and Professional Choices: A Hermeneutic Approach to Teaching Technical Communication." *Technical Communication Quarterly* 10, no. 1 (January 1, 2001): 97–116. https://doi.org/10.1207/s15427625tcq1001_4.

Twitter Help Center. "Making Images Accessible for People on Twitter." Accessed April 30, 2017. https://support.twitter.com/articles/20174660.

University of Exeter. "Types of Assessment: Definitions—Learning and Development." Accessed April 6, 2017. http://www.exeter.ac.uk/staff/development/academic/resources/assessment/principles/types/.

University of Vermont. "Guidelines and Principles: About UDL." 2017. https://www.uvm.edu/~cdci/universaldesign/?Page=about-udl/guidelines-principles.php&SM=about-udl/submenu.html.

University of Virginia. "Writing S.M.A.R.T. Goals." Accessed June 15, 2017. http://www.hr.virginia.edu/uploads/documents/media/Writing_SMART_Goals.pdf.

Usability.gov. "User Interface Design Basics." Accessed June 1, 2017. https://www.usability.gov/what-and-why/user-interface-design.html.

U.S. Access Board. "Overview of the Final Rule." January 2017. https://www.access-board.gov/guidelines-and-standards/communications-and-it/about-the-ict-refresh/overview-of-the-final-rule.

U.S. Department of Health and Human Services. "Tips on Using Design to Improve Readability." Agency for Healthcare Research and Quality, 2011. https://www.ahrq.gov/professionals/quality-patient-safety/talkingquality/resources/design/designreadability.html.

U.S. Department of Justice. "ADA Amendments Act of 2008." Federal Register, August 11, 2016. https://www.federalregister.gov/documents/2016/08/11/2016-17417/amendment-of-americans-with-disabilities-act-title-ii-and-title-iii-regulations-to-implement-ada.

———. "Federal and ADA Disability Resources." Information and Technical Assistance on the Americans with Disabilities Act, n.d. Accessed May 10, 2017. https://www.ada.gov/ada_fed_resources.htm.

———. "Justice Department Reaches Settlement with edX Inc., Provider of Massive Open Online Courses, to Make Its Website, Online Platform and Mobile Applications Accessible under the Americans with Disabilities Act." April 2, 2015. https://www.justice.gov/opa/pr/justice-department-reaches-settlement-edx-inc-provider-massive-open-online-courses-make-its.

U.S. Department of Justice. "2010 ADA Regulations." Information and Technical Assistance on the Americans with Disabilities Act, n.d. https://www.ada.gov/2010_regs.htm.

U.S. Equal Employment Opportunity Commission. "Americans with Disabilities Act Amendments Act of 2008." September 25, 2008. https://www.eeoc.gov/laws/statutes/adaaa.cfm.

Vimeo. "Captions and Subtitles." Help Center. Accessed August 8, 2017. https://help.vimeo.com/hc/en-us/articles/224968828-Captions-and-subtitles.

"VoiceOver Getting Started Guide." Accessed March 26, 2017. https://help.apple.com/voiceover/info/guide/10.12/.

Waterfield, Judith, Bob West, and Melanie Parker. "Supporting Inclusive Practice: Developing an Assessment Toolkit." In *Towards Inclusive Learning in Higher Education: Developing Curricula for Disabled Students*, edited by Mike Adams. New York: Routledge, 2006.

WebAIM. "Fonts." WebAIM. Center for Persons with Disabilities. Accessed April 4, 2017. http://webaim.org/techniques/fonts/.

———. "CSS in Action—Invisible Content Just for Screen Reader Users." Last updated December 11, 2014. Accessed August 3, 2017. http://webaim.org/techniques/css/invisiblecontent/.

———. "Link Text and Appearance." Links and Hypertext. Last updated October 3, 2013. http://webaim.org/techniques/hypertext/link_text.

———. "Motor Disabilities: Types of Motor Disabilities." October 12, 2012. http://webaim.org/articles/motor/motordisabilities.

———. "Visual Disabilities—Color-Blindness." August 28, 2013. http://webaim.org/articles/visual/colorblind.

WebbIE. "WebbIE, the Free Web Browser for Blind People with Little or No Sight." Accessed March 26, 2017. http://www.webbie.org.uk/.

Wegener, Debby. *Training Library Patrons the ADDIE Way*. New York: Elsevier, 2006.

Wildavsky, Aaron. *Speaking Truth to Power: The Art and Craft of Policy Analysis*. 2nd ed. New Brunswick, NJ: Transaction, 1987.

W3C. "About W3C." Accessed March 26, 2017. https://www.w3.org/Consortium/.

———. "Developing a Web Accessibility Business Case for Your Organization: Overview." Web Accessibility Initiative. September 7, 2012. https://www.w3.org/WAI/bcase/Overview.

———. "Introduction to Web Accessibility." Accessed March 26, 2017. https://www.w3.org/WAI/intro/accessibility.php.

———. "Understanding Success Criterion 1.4.2." Accessed April 15, 2017. https://www.w3.org/TR/UNDERSTANDING-WCAG20/visual-audio-contrast-dis-audio.html.

———. "Understanding Success Criterion 2.1.2." Accessed June 20, 2017. https://www.w3.org/TR/UNDERSTANDING-WCAG20/keyboard-operation-trapping.html.

———. "Using a Style Switcher to Provide a Conforming Alternate Version." 2016. https://www.w3.org/TR/WCAG20-TECHS/C29.html.

———. "Web Content Accessibility Guidelines (WCAG) Overview." March 10, 2017. https://www.w3.org/WAI/intro/wcag.

———. "Web Content Accessibility Guidelines (WCAG) 2.0." 2017. https://www.w3.org/TR/WCAG20/#meaning.

———. "Web Content Accessibility Guidelines (WCAG) 2.1." Accessed May 15, 2017. https://www.w3.org/TR/WCAG21/.

———. "W3C Working Draft 14 December 2016." WAI-ARIA Authoring Practices 1.1. December 14, 2016. https://www.w3.org/TR/wai-aria-practices/.

w3schools. "HTML Audio/Video DOM Reference." Accessed August 8, 2017. https://www.w3schools.com/tags/ref_av_dom.asp.

———. "HTML DOM Time Object." Accessed August 3, 2017. https://www.w3schools.com/jsref/dom_obj_time.asp.

———. "HTML5 Drag and Drop." Accessed August 10, 2017. https://www.w3schools.com/html/html5_draganddrop.asp.

———. "Understanding the Four Principles of Accessibility." Introduction to Understanding WCAG 2.0. 2016. https://www.w3.org/TR/UNDERSTANDING-WCAG20/intro.html#introduction-fourprincs-head.

———. "WebVTT: The Web Video Text Tracks Format." March 2017. https://w3c.github.io/webvtt/.

———. "World Wide Web Consortium (W3C)." 2017. https://www.w3.org/.

Wu, Xi Vivien, Mary Anne Heng, and Wenru Wang. "Nursing Students' Experiences with the Use of Authentic Assessment Rubric and Case Approach in the Clinical Laboratories." *Nurse Education Today* 35, no. 4 (April 2015): 549–55. https://doi.org/10.1016/j.nedt.2014.12.009.

Yick, Alice G. "Evaluating Readability of Domestic Violence Information Found on Domestic Violence State Coalitions' Websites." *Journal of Technology in Human Services* 26, no. 1 (January 2008): 67–75.

YouTube. "Supported Subtitle and Closed Caption Files." YouTube Help. Accessed April 30, 2017. https://support.google.com/youtube/answer/2734698?topic=3014331&ctx=topic.

———. "Use YouTube with a Screen Reader." YouTube Help. 2017. https://support.google.com/youtube/answer/189278?hl=en-GB.

———. "YouTube Now Defaults to HTML5 <video>." *YouTube Engineering and Developers Blog*. January 27, 2015. https://youtube-eng.googleblog.com/2015/01/youtube-now-defaults-to-html5_27.html.

Index

Page references for real-life scenarios are italicized.

About the Author

After a decade in corporate management, **Laura Francabandera** received her master's in library and information science from San Jose State University. She telecommutes from her home office as a learning systems technologist for Credo Education (Boston, MA)—implementing e-learning content into a variety of learning management systems in libraries and educational institutions. She passionately advocates for those who are often overlooked and for accessibility in all facets of technology. During her years at Credo Education, she spearheaded accessibility issues and overhauled the entire documentation program. She has spoken about technology and accessibility at library conferences across the country, as well as facilitated online webinars and in-person workshops. In her free time, she staffs the circulation desk at a university library, helping students locate information. Her curriculum vitae and other scholarship can be found at her website: https://francabandera.wordpress.com.

www.ingramcontent.com/pod-product-compliance
Ingram Content Group UK Ltd.
Pitfield, Milton Keynes, MK11 3LW, UK
UKHW051419150926
475561UK00005B/245

9 781538 108222